LENORMAND AROUND THE WORLD

How Culture and Belief Have Influenced the Lenormand System

ALEXANDRE MUSRUCK

4880 Lower Valley Road, Atglen, PA 19310

Other REDFeather Titles by the Author:
The Art of Lenormand Reading: Decoding Powerful Messages, ISBN 978-0-7643-5468-7
Lenormand Oracle Cards, ISBN 978-0-7643-5469-4
The Art of Kipper Reading: Decoding Powerful Messages, ISBN 978-0-7643-5901-9
Kipper Oracle Cards, ISBN 978-0-7643-5900-2

Library of Congress Control Number: 2025930659

Edited by Crystal Mannara
Designed by Beth Oberholtzer
Cover design by Danielle Farmer
Image credits: page 18, Portret van Johann Kaspar Hechtel (RP-P-1920-366, Lugt 2228); page 19, © The Trustees of the British Museum; pg 21, Woman reading the coffee grounds. Fortune-teller. Mysticism. Armenian coffee. (c)Javier Volcan, courtesy of shutterstock.com; page 51, courtesy of the Cleveland Museum of Art, CC0 public domain; page 61, © hyotographics, courtesy of Shutterstock

Type set in Elsie/Caecilia/Minion Pro/Helvetica Now

ISBN: 978-0-7643-7031-1
ePub: 978-1-5073-0592-8
Printed in India

10 9 8 7 6 5 4 3 2 1

Published by REDFeather Mind, Body, Spirit
An imprint of Schiffer Publishing, Ltd.
4880 Lower Valley Road
Atglen, PA 19310
Phone: (610) 593-1777; Fax: (610) 593-2002
Email: Info@redfeathermbs.com
Web: www.redfeathermbs.com

Content

CHAPTER 1

Introduction and About the Author

Dear readers,

If you've picked up this book, it's because you are eager to master the remarkable Lenormand oracle, a powerful and unique divination tool that, much like the Tarot, has captivated the world. I first began using the Lenormand deck as a young teenager, and my connection to it has only deepened and evolved with time. Over the years, I've had the privilege of sharing my passion for these cards through my many books and decks, now available in several languages. I consider myself incredibly fortunate. My love for the Lenormand has connected me with people from all corners of the globe who share the same enthusiasm for this oracle. Through these encounters, not only have I had the joy of teaching my approach, but I've also learned from others, gaining insights into how different cultures and traditions interpret and interact with the cards. This exchange of ideas and wisdom is what inspired the creation of this book.

Lenormand Around the World is not just a historical account of how the Lenormand system spread globally; it's a journey into the heart of how cultures, traditions, religions, and spiritual practices have breathed life into these cards over centuries. Through the pages of this book, you will

- understand the origins of Lenormand and how it became a worldwide phenomenon;

- explore the unique interpretations of the deck in various countries, from Europe to Latin America, Asia, the Creole Islands, and beyond;
- learn how tradition and spirituality have influenced the Lenormand cards and how they are interpreted differently on the basis of cultural beliefs;
- gain insights into the universal power of Lenormand to provide guidance, clarity, and answers in diverse spiritual practices; and
- unlock deeper meanings of the cards by understanding the cultural contexts in which they are used.

Whether you are a seasoned Lenormand reader or a curious beginner, this book will open your mind to the fascinating ways in which these cards serve as bridges between intuition, culture, and divination.

About the Author

Alexandre Musruck is a seasoned expert in the Lenormand card system and a passionate spiritual guide, deeply rooted in the traditions of his Creole ancestry. As the son and grandson of traditional Creole healers, Alexandre inherited a rich legacy of spiritual wisdom and practices that have shaped his journey as a healer and cartomancer. Living on the beautiful island of Réunion, Alexandre carries forth the ancestral knowledge of the Creole culture, blending it with his deep expertise in the Lenormand oracle to offer profound insights and guidance.

From a young age, Alexandre was immersed in the spiritual world, learning the healing arts, divination, and sacred rituals passed down through generations. His upbringing on Réunion Island, a cultural crossroads among African, Indian, and European influences, instilled in him a deep understanding of the spiritual diversity that shapes his work today. This unique blend of traditions allows Alexandre to approach the Lenormand system with a rare depth of insight, infusing each reading with the wisdom of his ancestors.

As an authority on the Lenormand deck, Alexandre is renowned for his ability to unravel its complexities, providing readings that offer both practical guidance and spiritual enlightenment. His expertise spans beyond fortune-telling, since he integrates magical rituals, prayers, and sacred practices into his work with the cards. Alexandre has made it his mission

to preserve and teach the Lenormand tradition, while also exploring its synchronicities with Catholic saints and Hindu deities, bridging different spiritual systems for those seeking deeper, more-meaningful connections with the divine.

Through his teachings, readings, and spiritual services, Alexandre Musruck continues to empower individuals on their paths, offering healing, clarity, and guidance with the same dedication his Creole ancestors practiced.

CHAPTER 2

What Is the Lenormand Oracle?

Before exploring its journey, let's take a moment to understand what a Lenormand deck is and what makes it such a powerful tool for divination.

The Lenormand deck is a system of thirty-six cards, each bearing a simple image such as a tree, a fox, or a star. While these symbols may seem ordinary at first glance, they hold layers of meaning and power. What distinguishes Lenormand from other card systems, such as Tarot, is its directness and practicality. The cards are read in combinations, creating straightforward messages that can answer questions about love, work, health, and life in general.

A brief "GENERAL" overview of each Lenormand card:

1. Rider:
News, messages, or an arrival

2. Clovers:
Luck, opportunities, or small gains

3. Ship:
Travel, movement, or exploration

4. House:
Home, family, or stability

5. Tree:
Health, growth, or ancestry

6. Clouds:
Confusion, uncertainty, or temporary issues

7. Snake:
Deception, challenges, or transformation

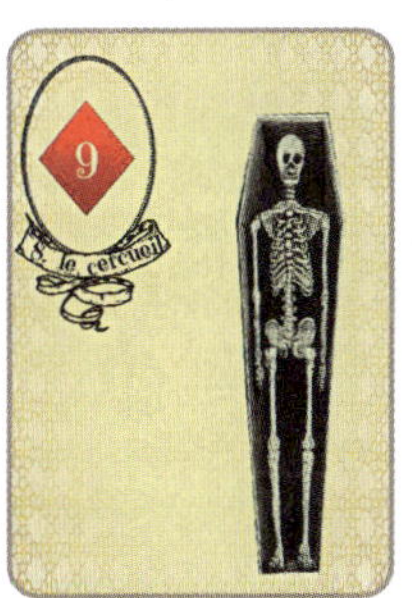

8. Coffin:
Endings, transitions, or transformation

9. Bouquet:
Gifts, happiness, or beauty

10. Scythe:
Sudden changes, decisions, or cutting away

11. Whip:
Conflict, arguments, or repetition

12. Birds:
Communication, gossip, or social interactions

13. Child:
New beginnings, innocence,
or a younger person

14. Fox:
Cunning, deception,
or work-related matters

15. Bear:
Strength, power,
or financial matters

16. Stars:
Hope, inspiration,
or guidance

17. Stork:
Change, movement,
or transitions

18. Dog:
Loyalty, friendship,
or support

19. Tower:
Authority, isolation,
or institutions

20. Garden:
Social events, public life,
or gatherings

21. Mountain:
Obstacles, challenges,
or delays

22. Crossroad:
Choices, decisions,
or paths

23. Mice:
Loss, stress,
or small troubles

24. Heart:
Love, emotions,
or relationships

25. Ring:
Commitments, partnerships, or contracts

26. Book:
Secrets, knowledge, or learning

27. Letter:
Messages, documents, or communication

28. Man:
A significant man or masculine energy

29. Woman:
A significant woman or feminine energy

30. Lily:
Peace, maturity, or spirituality

31. Sun:
Success, vitality,
or positivity

32. Moon:
Emotions, intuition,
or cycles

33. Key:
Solutions, success,
or important answers

34. Fish:
Wealth, abundance,
or business

35. Anchor:
Stability, security,
or a firm foundation

36. Cross:
Burdens, trials,
or spiritual lessons

A Sample Reading

Question: What can I expect in my career over the next month?

Drawn Cards:

1. Ship (3): Movement or travel related to work
2. Fox (14): Work-related issues or challenges
3. Anchor (35): Stability and security

Answer: The Ship card suggests that there will be movement or changes in your career this month, possibly involving travel or new opportunities. The Fox card indicates that you may encounter some challenges or deceptive situations at work. It's a reminder to stay alert and cautious about office politics or hidden agendas. However, the Anchor card offers reassurance that despite any difficulties, you will maintain stability and security in your career. It's a positive sign that any disruptions will ultimately lead to a more secure and grounded position.

Unlike the abstract and often-mystical symbolism of Tarot, Lenormand offers concise, almost literal interpretations. If Tarot is the map of the soul, Lenormand is the compass for daily life, offering clear insights into immediate situations. Lenormand doesn't dance around the question. Its directness allows for fast, actionable insights, making it a favorite tool for those who seek clarity in the present moment. Although each card carries a straightforward image, they provide a profound message when combined. This makes Lenormand accessible but, at the same time, layered in meaning. Lenormand speaks to everyday situations. It's known for its ability to give precise answers to practical questions, which makes it a powerful tool for navigating life's complexities.

CHAPTER 3

The Origins of Lenormand

Understanding the Concept of Schools in Lenormand

In the world of Lenormand readings, the concept of "schools" refers to the various interpretations and methodologies that have emerged over time and across different cultures. These schools reflect the unique historical, cultural, and spiritual contexts in which the Lenormand deck has been utilized. As such, they contribute to the rich tapestry of meanings associated with each card and influence how readers approach their practice. Understanding the diversity of card interpretations from various schools will enhance your readings and foster a deeper connection to the rich history and cultural significance of the Lenormand tradition.

Origins and Naming of the Lenormand

Johannes Kaspar Hechtel, also known as J. K. Hechtel, was a German inventor credited with designing the Lenormand deck known as the Game of Hope, or "Das Spiel der Hoffnung." First published in 1799, the deck was intentionally named after Marie Anne Lenormand, a renowned French clairvoyant and cartomancer. Lenormand was celebrated for her exceptional card-reading skills and her connections with prominent figures of her era. Her fame in France and her impact on the practice of cartomancy contributed to the deck being named in her honor. As a result, the Lenormand deck gained widespread recognition and popularity in French-speaking regions. It is important to note that Adélaide never used Hechtel's deck, since it was created after her death. The cards she used were certainly playing cards—a piquet deck of thirty-two cards with annotations and traditional Tarot cards.

Germany, "the Birthplace"

Johann Kaspar Hechtel, the German inventor and card maker, is often credited as the father of the Petit Lenormand deck. However, Hechtel's association with the famous French fortune-teller Mademoiselle Marie Anne Lenormand was a clever marketing strategy that inaccurately linked his creation to her reputation. Though Mademoiselle Lenormand gained fame for her fortune-telling skills and had a deep influence on the practice of cartomancy, she never used Hechtel's deck. Instead, Hechtel, through his 1799 creation known as the "Game of Hope," laid the foundation for what would later become the Petit Lenormand deck.

Born in Nuremberg, Hechtel was a polymath with interests in literature, mathematics, and card games. His creation, "the Game of Hope," was not initially intended as a divination tool. It was a parlor game for entertainment, with players moving tokens around a board of thirty-six cards, each adorned with symbolic images such as the Rider, House, and Tree. These symbols, meant to tell fortunes during gameplay, would eventually become the basis for the Petit Lenormand deck. Hechtel's marketing move to associate his game with Marie Anne Lenormand was astute. Lenormand had risen to fame as a cartomancer, gaining notable clientele that included influential figures such as Napoleon Bonaparte and Empress Josephine. Hechtel's deck, falsely attributed as Mademoiselle Lenormand's personal oracle, quickly gained

popularity in France, helping establish the Petit Lenormand deck as a divination tool.

One of the influences on Hechtel's creation of the Petit Lenormand deck can be traced back to coffee ground reading, also known as tasseography.

Lady Charlotte Schreiber's Collection and the British Museum

The historical significance of early Lenormand decks can be seen in the collections of Lady Charlotte Schreiber, an avid collector of playing cards in the nineteenth century. Her extensive collection includes many early cartomancy decks, including early versions of the Lenormand. These cards are now housed at the British Museum, where they offer a glimpse into the origins and evolution of the deck. Lady Schreiber's collection features rare editions of the Game of Hope and early Lenormand decks, showcasing the transition from a simple game to a powerful divination tool. Her efforts in preserving these items contribute greatly to our understanding of the Petit Lenormand's development.

The Vienna Coffee Cards: Inspiration Behind the Lenormand Oracle

The Vienna Coffee Cards are believed to have been a significant inspiration for the creation of the Lenormand oracle. Dating back to 1796, just three years earlier than the famed Game of Hope, these cards offered a novel approach to fortune-telling that merged symbols and advice to guide querents in divining their future. The deck, composed of thirty-two cards, was notably similar in many ways to the later Lenormand cards, with familiar imagery such as the Clover, House, Heart, and Key, among others. However, the Vienna Coffee Cards also included unique symbols such as a Lion and the Bugs, adding further layers of interpretation and meaning.

Printed on each card was guidance for the querent, offering specific advice or interpretations for the card drawn. Much like the Lenormand oracle, the aim was to deliver clear, actionable insights about the querent's future, making the Coffee Cards an invaluable tool in cartomantic practices.

At the heart of the Vienna Coffee Cards is the practice of tasseomancy, a form of divination that uses the residual shapes left behind by coffee grounds or tea leaves in a cup. This ancient practice, with origins in both the Middle East and China, eventually spread throughout Europe, becoming particularly popular in Vienna's coffeehouses during the late eighteenth century. Tasseomancy, sometimes referred to as coffee ground reading, served as a spiritual ritual, a way for people to decode hidden messages from the natural patterns that appeared at the bottom of their cups.

The Art of Coffee Ground Reading

Traditionally, the querent would drink a cup of strong coffee or tea, leaving a small amount of liquid at the bottom. For coffee, especially in Middle Eastern tradition, this would often be a thick brew such as Turkish coffee that left a considerable residue of grounds. The querent swirls the cup gently, ensuring that the grounds or leaves spread and coat the sides of the cup. Once this condition is satisfied, the cup is then turned upside down onto a saucer, allowing the excess liquid to drain while the grounds or leaves settle into distinct patterns.

The tasseographer (reader) then examines the shapes formed by the coffee grounds or tea leaves. These shapes can resemble various symbols, animals, letters, or even numbers. Each shape carries a different meaning. For example, a heart might signify love or a new romantic opportunity, while a snake could represent treachery or hidden dangers. The reader uses these shapes, along with their intuitive understanding, to provide a forecast of the querent's future. The placement of the shapes within the cup can also be significant, with different areas representing different aspects of the querent's life (e.g., love, career, health).

The Vienna Coffee Cards likely evolved as a tool for those who enjoyed the practice of tasseomancy but desired a quicker, more accessible way to divine their future. Rather than reading patterns in a cup, one could simply draw a card, each of which contained symbols and advice akin to those seen in coffee ground readings. The cards thus combined the mystical world of tasseomancy with the convenience and clarity of cartomancy.

This hybridization of tasseomancy and cartomancy can be seen in the detailed artwork and symbolism on the Vienna Coffee Cards. Each card was designed to mimic the evocative imagery found in coffee grounds, offering both direct and intuitive insights. Like when reading the patterns in a cup, the reader of the Vienna Coffee Cards was guided to interpret both the symbols and the accompanying printed advice to forecast the querent's future.

Many of the familiar Lenormand symbols—such as the Clover, Cross, Fox, and Sun—are believed to have been directly inspired by the images on the Vienna Coffee Cards. The deck of thirty-two cards shares much with the thirty-six-card Lenormand deck, with just a few additional symbols being added or changed in the later version.

However, the key difference lies in the systems' origins. The Vienna Coffee Cards were more deeply rooted in the practice of tasseomancy, while the Lenormand oracle, which came later, borrowed elements of German and French cartomantic traditions. Still, the basic premise—using symbolic imagery to offer direct advice about life, love, and fortune—remained constant between the two systems.

In the years that followed, the Vienna Coffee Cards were largely overshadowed by the Lenormand system, which gained widespread popularity across Europe. But for many cartomancers, the Vienna Coffee Cards represent an essential link in the history of divination, blending the ancient practices of tasseomancy with the cartomantic traditions that would follow.

Thus, the Vienna Coffee Cards not only inspired the creation of the Lenormand oracle but also stand as a testament to the enduring appeal of divination through symbols—whether read in the grounds of a coffee cup or the cards of a deck.

CHAPTER 4

The German Way of Reading Lenormand

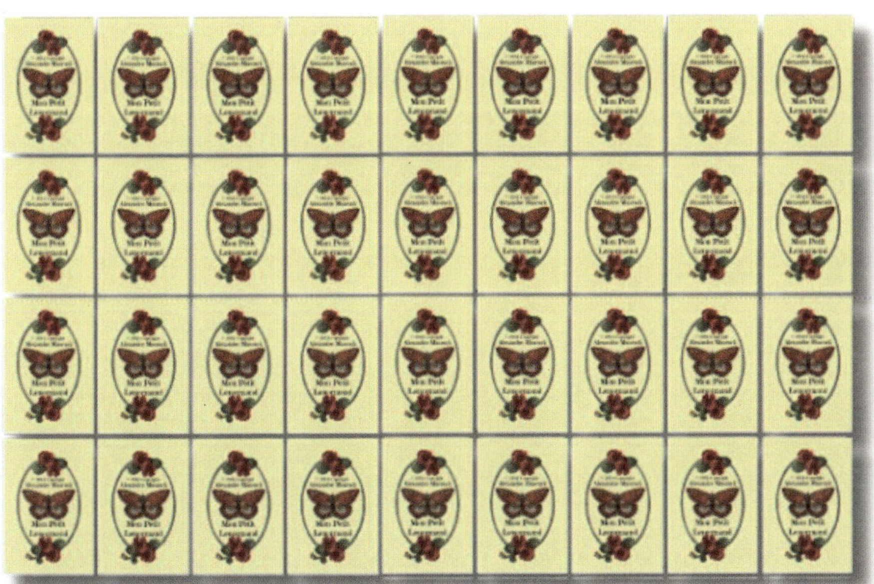

Though the Lenormand system is widely known today, the German style of reading differs in some key ways from its French counterpart. German cartomancers focus heavily on practical, straightforward interpretations, and their reading methods emphasize the context of nearby cards, distance within the spread, and directional clues. Let's explore the unique German methods in more detail:

The Method de Distance (Near & Far)

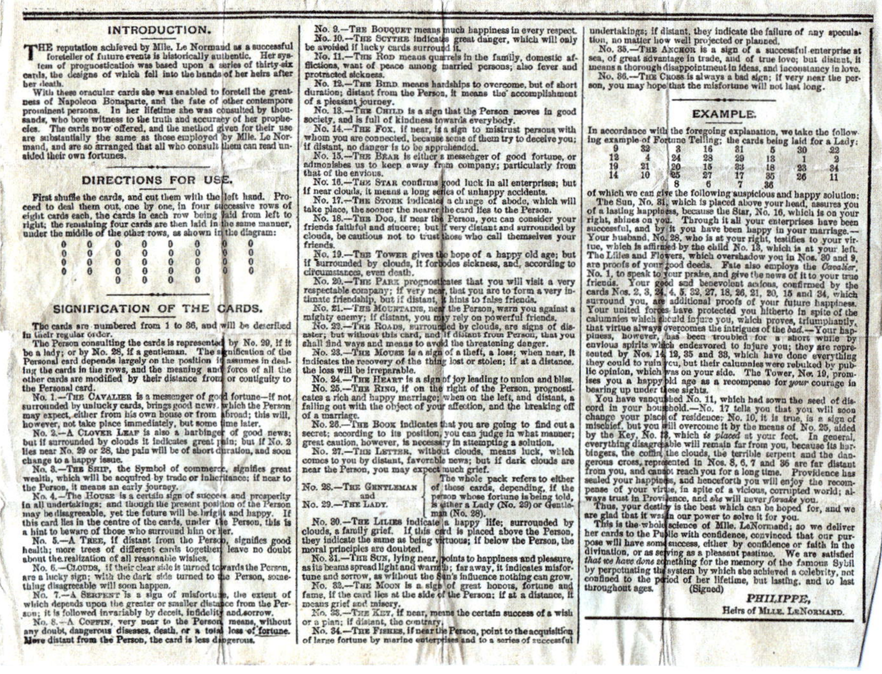

INTRODUCTION.

THE reputation achieved by Mlle. Le Normand as a successful foreteller of future events is historically authentic. Her system of prognostication was based upon a series of thirty-six cards, the designs of which fell into the hands of her heirs after her death.

With these oracular cards she was enabled to foretell the greatness of Napoleon Bonaparte, and the fate of other contempore prominent persons. In her lifetime she was consulted by thousands, who bore witness to the truth and accuracy of her prophecies. The cards now offered, and the method given for their use are substantially the same as those employed by Mlle. Le Normand, and are so arranged that all who consult them can read unaided their own fortunes.

DIRECTIONS FOR USE.

First shuffle the cards, and cut them with the left hand. Proceed to deal them out, one by one, in four successive rows of eight cards each, the cards in each row being laid from left to right; the remaining four cards are then laid in the same manner, under the middle of the other rows, as shown in the diagram:

0	0	0	0	0	0	0	0
0	0	0	0	0	0	0	0
0	0	0	0	0	0	0	0
0	0	0	0	0	0	0	0
		0	0	0	0		

SIGNIFICATION OF THE CARDS.

The cards are numbered from 1 to 36, and will be described in their regular order.

The Person consulting the cards is represented by No. 29, if it be a lady; or by No. 28, if a gentleman. The signification of the Personal card depends largely on the position it assumes in dealing the cards in the rows, and the meaning and force of all the other cards are modified by their distance from or contiguity to the Personal card.

No. 1.—The Cavalier is a messenger of good fortune—if not surrounded by unlucky cards, brings good news, which the Person may expect, either from his own house or from abroad; this will, however, not take place immediately, but some time later.

No. 2.—A Clover Leaf is also a harbinger of good news; but if surrounded by clouds it indicates great pain; but if No. 2 lies near No. 29 or 28, the pain will be of short duration, and soon change to a happy issue.

No. 3.—The Ship, the Symbol of commerce, signifies great wealth, which will be acquired by trade or inheritance; if near to the Person, it means an early journey.

No. 4.—The House is a certain sign of success and prosperity in all undertakings; and though the present position of the Person may be disagreeable, yet the future will be bright and happy. If this card lies in the centre of the cards, under the Person, this is a hint to beware of those who surround him or her.

No. 5.—A Tree, if distant from the Person, signifies good health; more trees of different cards together leave no doubt about the realization of all reasonable wishes.

No. 6.—Clouds, if their clear side is turned towards the Person, are a lucky sign; with the dark side turned to the Person, something disagreeable will soon happen.

No. 7.—A Serpent is a sign of misfortune, the extent of which depends upon the greater or smaller distance from the Person; it is followed invariably by deceit, infidelity and sorrow.

No. 8.—A Coffin, very near to the Person means, without any doubt, dangerous diseases, death, or a total loss of fortune. More distant from the Person, the card is less dangerous.

No. 9.—The Bouquet means much happiness in every respect.

No. 10.—The Scythe indicates great danger, which will only be avoided if lucky cards surround it.

No. 11.—The Rod means quarrels in the family, domestic afflictions, want of peace among married persons; also fever and protracted sickness.

No. 12.—The Bird means hardships to overcome, but of short duration; distant from the Person, it means the accomplishment of a pleasant journey.

No. 13.—The Child is a sign that the Person moves in good society, and is full of kindness towards everybody.

No. 14.—The Fox, if near, is a sign to mistrust persons with whom you are connected, because some of them try to deceive you; if distant, no danger is to be apprehended.

No. 15.—The Bear is either a messenger of good fortune, or admonishes us to keep away from company; particularly from that of the envious.

No. 16.—The Star confirms good luck in all enterprises; but if near clouds, it means a long series of unhappy accidents.

No. 17.—The Stork indicates a change of abode, which will take place, the sooner the nearer the card lies to the Person.

No. 18.—The Dog, if near the Person, you can consider your friends faithful and sincere; but if very distant and surrounded by clouds, be cautious not to trust those who call themselves your friends.

No. 19.—The Tower gives the hope of a happy old age; but if surrounded by clouds, it forbodes sickness, and, according to circumstances, even death.

No. 20.—The Park prognosticates that you will visit a very respectable company; if very near, that you are to form a very intimate friendship, but if distant, it hints to false friends.

No. 21.—The Mountains, near the Person, warn you against a mighty enemy; if distant, you may rely on powerful friends.

No. 22.—The Roads, surrounded by clouds, are signs of disaster; but without this card, and if distant from Person, that you shall find ways and means to avoid the threatening danger.

No. 23.—The Mouse is a sign of a theft, a loss; when near, it indicates the recovery of the thing lost or stolen; if at a distance, the loss will be irreparable.

No. 24.—The Heart is a sign of joy leading to union and bliss.

No. 25.—The Ring, if on the right of the Person, prognosticates a rich and happy marriage; when on the left, and distant, a falling out with the object of your affection, and the breaking off of a marriage.

No. 26.—The Book indicates that you are going to find out a secret; according to its position, you can judge in what manner; great caution, however, is necessary in attempting a solution.

No. 27.—The Letter, without clouds, means luck, which comes to you by distant, favorable news; but if dark clouds are near the Person, you may expect much grief.

No. 28.—The Gentleman and No. 29.—The Lady. } The whole pack refers to either of these cards, depending, if the person whose fortune is being told, is either a Lady (No. 29) or Gentleman (No. 28).

No. 30.—The Lilies indicate a happy life; surrounded by clouds, a family grief. If this card is placed above the Person, they indicate the same as being virtuous; if below the Person, the moral principles are doubted.

No. 31.—The Sun, lying near, points to happiness and pleasure, as its beams spread light and warmth; far away, it indicates misfortune and sorrow, as without the Sun's influence nothing can grow.

No. 32.—The Moon is a sign of great honors, fortune and fame, if the card lies at the side of the Person; if at a distance, it means grief and misery.

No. 33.—The Key, if near, means the certain success of a wish or a plan; if distant, the contrary.

No. 34.—The Fishes, if near the Person, point to the acquisition of large fortune by marine enterprises and to a series of successful undertakings; if distant, they indicate the failure of any speculation, no matter how well projected or planned.

No. 35.—The Anchor is a sign of a successful enterprise at sea, of great advantage in trade, and of true love; but distant, it means a thorough disappointment in ideas, and inconstancy in love.

No. 36.—The Cross is always a bad sign; if very near the person, you may hope that the misfortune will not last long.

EXAMPLE.

In accordance with the foregoing explanation, we take the following example of Fortune Telling; the cards being laid for a Lady:

9	32	3	16	31	5	30	22
12	4	24	28	29	13	1	2
19	21	20	15	33	18	23	34
14	10	25	27	17	35	26	11
		8	6	7	36		

of which we can give the following auspicious and happy solution:

The Sun, No. 31, which is placed above your head, assures you of a lasting happiness, because the Star, No. 16, which is on your right, shines on you. Through it all your enterprises have been successful, and by it you have been happy in your marriage.—Your husband, No. 28, who is at your right, testifies to your virtue, which is affirmed by the child No. 13, which is at your left. The Lilies and Flowers, which overshadow you in Nos. 30 and 9, are proofs of your good deeds. Fate also employs the *Cavalier*, No. 1, to speak to your praise, and give the news of it to your true friends. Your good and benevolent actions, confirmed by the cards Nos. 2, 3, 24, 4, 5, 32, 27, 18, 26, 21, 20, 15 and 34, which surround you, are additional proofs of your future happiness. Your united forces have protected you hitherto in spite of the calumnies which should injure you, which proves, triumphantly, that virtue always overcomes the intrigues of the *bad*.—Your happiness, however, has been troubled for a short while by envious spirits which endeavored to injure you; they are represented by Nos. 14, 12, 35 and 33, which have done everything they could to ruin you, but their calumnies were rebuked by public opinion, which was on your side. The Tower, No. 19, promises you a happy old age as a recompense for *your* courage in bearing up under these sights.

You have vanquished No. 11, which had sown the seed of discord in your household.—No. 17 tells you that you will soon change your place of residence; No. 10, it is true, is a sign of mischief, but you will overcome it by the means of No. 25, aided by the Key, No. 33, which *is placed* at your feet. In general, everything disagreeable will remain far from you, because its harbingers, the coffin, the clouds, the terrible serpent and the dangerous cross, represented in Nos. 8, 6, 7 and 36 are far distant from you, and cannot reach you for a long time. Providence has sealed your happiness, and henceforth you will enjoy the recompense of your virtue, in spite of a vicious, corrupted world; always trust in Providence, and *she* will never *forsake* you.

Thus, your destiny is the best which can be hoped for, and we are glad that it was in our power to solve it for you.

This is the whole science of Mlle. LeNormand; so we deliver her cards to the Public with confidence, convinced that our purpose will have some success, either by confidence or faith in the divination, or as serving as a pleasant pastime. We are satisfied *that we have done something* for the memory of the famous Sybil by perpetuating the system by which she achieved a celebrity, not confined to the period of her lifetime, but lasting, and to last throughout ages.

(Signed)

PHILIPPE,

Heirs of Mlle. LeNormand.

The origins of the Méthode de Distance can be traced back to a single page of keyword meanings and interpretive guidance included in early versions of the Lenormand deck. This leaflet was purportedly authored by Philippe Lenormand, a fictional character created by the deck's publishers to enhance the credibility of the system. While Philippe was said to be Mlle. Lenormand's late nephew, he was, in reality, a fabrication designed to boost the appeal of the Lenormand deck and method.

Despite its origins in marketing, the Méthode de Distance has become one of the most enduring and widely used techniques in Lenormand practice. The Method of Distance was originally conceived for use in the Grand Tableau—a thirty-six-card spread where all the cards are laid out in four rows of nine cards each, which may correspond to the fact that the Lenormand deck consists of nine cards from each of the four suits in a standard French playing-card deck: hearts, diamonds, clubs, and spades. This layout provides a bird's-eye view of the querent's life, with each card representing different aspects of their present, past, and future. The Grand Tableau offers a vast amount of information, and the Méthode de Distance serves as a tool for narrowing down which influences are most relevant to the querent. The significator card, representing the querent, is key to the Méthode de Distance. Traditionally, the significator is card 28 (the Man) for male querents and card 29 (the Woman) for female querents. The significator is the point of reference for the rest of the cards in the spread. The distance of other cards from the significator determines their influence on the querent's life, with those closest to the significator holding the strongest sway. The Méthode de Distance treats the Grand Tableau as a map, with the significator at its center. The cards surrounding the significator represent the people, events, and circumstances that are currently influencing the querent. The closer a card is to the significator, the stronger and more immediate its impact. Conversely, the farther a card is, the weaker or more delayed its influence.

a) Close Cards (One to Three Cards Away)

Cards within one to three spaces of the significator have the most direct and powerful effect on the querent's life. These are events, people, or emotions that are currently active and demand the querent's immediate attention.For example:

- The Ring card (25), if located within one to three cards of the significator, would suggest a strong focus on relationships, commitments, or contracts that are currently influencing the querent's life.
- The Mountain card (21) in proximity would indicate immediate obstacles or challenges the querent must face.

b) Middle Distance (Four to Six Cards Away)

Cards positioned four to six spaces from the significator reflect influences that, while significant, are not yet fully realized or are slightly removed from the querent's immediate sphere. These influences are still relevant but may not require immediate action. For example:

- The Fish card (34) at this distance might suggest that financial matters are of concern, but they are not yet critical or urgent. These issues are on the horizon but not the current focus.
- The Garden card (20) could point to upcoming social events, public gatherings, or community interactions that will soon become relevant to the querent's situation.

c) Far Distance (Seven or More Cards Away)

Cards farther than seven spaces from the significator indicate distant or future influences. These are situations or people that the querent may not yet be aware of, or they represent long-term developments. For example:

- The Ship card (3) located far from the significator may indicate distant travel, long-term goals, or distant opportunities that will come to fruition in time but are not yet in play.
- The Cross card (36) at a distance is a good omen, indicating that things will improve and that relief is on the horizon for the querent.

In the method of distance, negative cards such as the Coffin, Clouds, or Cross (which I call the 'three C's') can actually be seen as favorable, as their

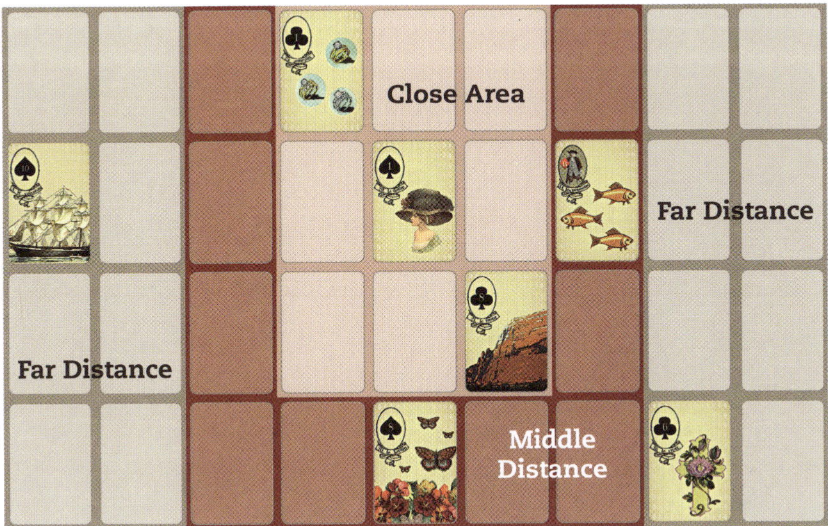

negative influence does not impact the querent's life directly. On the other hand, when positive cards like the Clover, the Key, or the Sun appear far from the querent, it implies that they may be facing challenging times or that blessings are out of reach for now.

Diagonal Influences

In addition to the proximity of cards in a vertical or horizontal direction, the cards located diagonally from the significator are also significant in the Méthode de Distance. Diagonal cards often represent hidden influences, subconscious emotions, or underlying factors that subtly shape the querent's experiences. For example:

- If the Book card (26) appears diagonally, it could indicate hidden knowledge, secrets, or undisclosed information that will influence the querent's situation.
- A diagonal Fox card (14) might suggest cunning or deceptive actions taking place behind the scenes, hinting at manipulations the querent is not yet aware of.

From the Grand Tableau to Smaller Spreads

At the beginning of my Lenormand practice, I adhered closely to the rule of dealing the Grand Tableau for every question. However, I quickly found that this method, while thorough, could be time consuming. Over time, I noticed that not every card in the Grand Tableau needed to be read in order to answer a querent's question. Instead, I found myself naturally extracting specific portions of the spread that directly addressed the question at hand. This was a game changer in my practice. By recognizing that smaller sections of the Grand Tableau could provide the same level of insight, I began experimenting with condensed layouts such as lines of three, five, or seven cards. This allowed me to maintain the core principle of proximity that defines the Method de Distance, while significantly reducing the time spent spreading out all thirty-six cards.

One of the most significant benefits of using small spreads is the ability to answer more questions in less time, without sacrificing accuracy or depth. By focusing on smaller spreads, I can deliver concise readings with the same level of confidence and insight as the Grand Tableau, allowing me to meet the needs of more clients or address multiple queries in a shorter amount of time.

Small Spreads: String or a Run

These smaller spreads still maintain the core concept of proximity from the Méthode de Distance. The closer a card is to the querent (or significator), the stronger its influence, even in a limited number of cards. Below are some examples of how these spreads work:

a) Line of Three

The three-card spread is a simple and quick way to gain clarity. The center card always serves as the focal point, representing the core of the situation. The two side cards provide context or further details, with the final card acting as the answer or the concluding note, bringing the reading to a clear resolution.

b) Line of Five

The five-card spread offers the simplicity of the three-card spread, but with added depth and detail. The central card remains the focal point, while the surrounding four cards provide context. Cards to the left represent past influences or current circumstances, while those to the right point to future outcomes or what is yet to unfold. I view this spread as a snapshot, offering a fresh perspective on a situation and revealing new insights.

c) Line of Seven

The seven-card spread is particularly intriguing because it combines two sets of triplet cards on either side of a central focus card. Starting from the left, the first group of three cards sheds light on the recent past, revealing what the client has been going through. The middle card serves as the focus, highlighting what is happening in the present moment. The final group of three cards on the right points to the outcome, offering advice, solutions, or the result.

The Nine-Card Spread: Boxing the Querent

Among all the small spreads, the nine-card spread remains one of my personal favorites due to its balance between detail and simplicity. This spread, arranged in a three-by-three grid, is like a mini version of the Grand Tableau. The central card represents the querent or the main issue, while the eight surrounding cards offer insight into the various influences surrounding them, effectively "boxing" the querent in much the same way as the Grand Tableau does.

In this spread, proximity is key. With the significator at center, those cards positioned top/bottom and left/right are the most influential, while those in the outer corners may represent broader or more-distant factors. By analyzing the relationship between these cards, I can offer a comprehensive analysis of the querent's situation without the need for a full thirty-six-card spread.

Directional Clues

In the German style of Lenormand readings, the concept of directionality holds significant importance. This technique involves interpreting the orientation of the cards in relation to the querent, focusing on how the cards face them and their implications for the reading. The directional clues derived from this practice can provide deeper insights into the querent's situation, guiding the reader in delivering more-accurate predictions and advice.

The Significance of Directionality:

The Blessing Above: A Card of Favor

When a card appears directly above the querent in a Lenormand spread, its significance becomes amplified. If this card holds a positive meaning, it acts as a blessing, showering the querent with favorable energies, opportunities, and insights. For example, if the Bouquet card—a symbol of joy, beauty, and abundance—appears above the querent, it heralds a time of happiness and recognition. The querent may find themselves receiving compliments, experiencing unexpected joys, or enjoying the fruits of their labor.

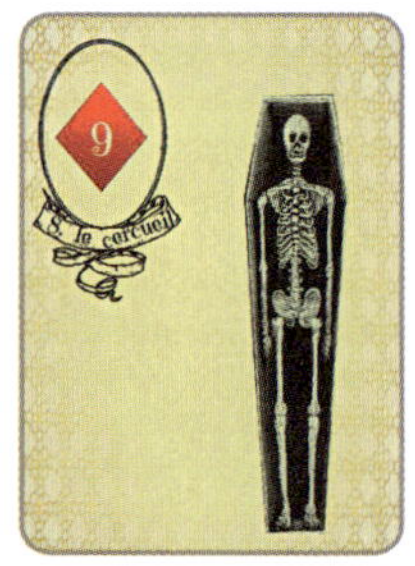

Conversely, when a card with negative connotations occupies this position, it can cast a shadow over the querent, functioning as a curse. For instance, if the Coffin card, which represents endings and loss, appears above the querent, it signals a time of mourning or the conclusion of a significant chapter. This positioning often indicates that the querent may be unwittingly inviting or intensifying these negative influences into their life, serving as a reminder to take heed of their surroundings and choices. We can also see this position as the mind, what the querent is focusing, or on what is not yet materialized.

The Ground Beneath: Mastery and Understanding

The cards situated directly beneath the querent—what they metaphorically walk on—represent knowledge and mastery that the querent possesses or clings to. These cards often reveal what the querent has already navigated or what influences their current situation. For example, if the Tree card, symbolizing health and ancestral roots, lies beneath the querent, it suggests a deep understanding of their familial or spiritual legacy. This knowledge can empower them, enabling them to draw strength from their past experiences as they face new challenges.

On the other hand, if the Mice card appears beneath the querent, it could signify an awareness of loss, anxiety, or decay. This card may indicate that the querent is holding on to past grievances or fears that are subtly undermining their confidence and progress. Recognizing the influences of these cards can guide the querent in understanding how their past shapes their present and can illuminate paths to healing and growth.

The Cause Behind: Understanding Origins

The cards positioned behind (to the left of) the querent reveal the underlying causes of their current situation. These cards symbolize past experiences, decisions, and events that have led to the present moment. For instance, if the Snake card—often associated with deception or transformation—lies behind the querent, it may point to past betrayals or lessons learned the hard way. This understanding of origins can empower the querent to release past burdens, recognize patterns, and make informed choices moving forward.

Conversely, if the Sun card, representing success and positivity, appears behind the querent, it suggests that the querent has recently experienced triumphs that continue to positively influence their current situation. This positioning reminds the querent of their capacity for success and encourages them to harness that energy in facing challenges.

The Effect Ahead: Projections into the Future

Finally, the cards that appear in front of the querent symbolize the potential effects of their current actions and choices. These cards can serve as a compass, guiding the querent toward the outcomes that lie ahead. If the Star card, representing hope and guidance, is positioned in front of the querent, it heralds a time of clarity and positivity, suggesting that the querent is on the right path. This card encourages the querent to embrace their intuition and trust in the journey ahead.

Conversely, if the Cross card, symbolizing burdens and challenges, appears in front of the querent, it may indicate that they are heading toward a period of trial or difficulty. This awareness can inspire proactive measures, prompting the querent to prepare mentally and spiritually for the obstacles they may encounter.

In addition to positional meanings, the concept of directionality plays a crucial role in interpreting Lenormand readings, particularly in the German style. This technique involves analyzing the orientation of the cards in relation to the querent, focusing on how the cards face them and their implications for the reading.

- Facing the querent: Cards that face the querent are considered auspicious and hold positive implications. They represent opportunities, potential, and favorable outcomes that are currently within the querent's reach. This direction signifies the future, suggesting what is to come or what the querent should embrace moving forward. For example, if the Ship card appears facing the querent, it indicates upcoming journeys, exploration, or new ventures.

- Turning away from the querent: In contrast, cards that turn away from the querent are interpreted as less favorable. These cards may signify obstacles, challenges, or past experiences that the querent needs to overcome or learn from. This directional aspect emphasizes that what is behind the querent represents the past, highlighting influences that may still affect their current situation but are no longer beneficial. If the Fox card, often associated with cunning and deceit, is facing away from the querent, it may indicate that they are moving away from past manipulations but need to remain vigilant.

THE GAME OF HOPE, from Board Game to Divination Tool

It is widely believed that the Lenormand deck was originally conceived as a board game, with its structure and gameplay serving as the foundation for what would later evolve into this popular tool for divination.

How to Play

Before starting the game, each player must make a deposit of six to eight marks to create a prize pool. The mark was the German currency used until 1999, after which it was replaced by the euro. Of course, you can replace the marks with board game money, poker chips, or any other object that can represent winnings.

The thirty-six cards of the Petit Lenormand are arranged in ascending order (from the Rider, card 1, to the Cross, card 36) in a six-by-six grid to form the game board. Each player takes turns rolling the dice and moves their token from square to square according to the result. As they advance, they will encounter various symbols that will be positive, negative, or neutral. The first player to reach House 35, the Anchor, wins. Some squares are special, such as the Coffin square: As in Monopoly's jail square, when you land here, you lose a turn until you roll doubles or another player lands on this square, freeing you.

Specific rules for the Game of Hope squares:

- Square 3, House of the Ship: The player who rolls a 3 arrives at the Ship, which will take them to the Island of Birds on square 12.
- Square 4, the House square: Upon arriving at the house, you must pay two marks to the doorman.
- Square 6, House of the Clouds: Upon arriving here, you are taken to square 2, the Clover.
- Square 7, House of the Snake: To avoid the snake's bite, the player landing here must pay two marks.
- Square 8, House of the Coffin: The player loses a turn until they roll doubles or another player is trapped in the coffin.
- Square 11, House of the Whip: To escape the whip's lashes, the player must pay two marks to safely reach the Child's House on square 13.
- Square 14, House of the Fox: The cunning fox forces the player who arrives at his house to hide in the woods on square 5, which is the Tree House.
- Square 16, House of the Star: Upon reaching the star, the player is rewarded with six marks.
- Square 21, House of the Mountain: As with House 8, the Coffin, the player loses a turn until they roll doubles or another player gets trapped here.
- Square 22, House of the Paths: The paths lead you to a playful and welcoming place, square 20, the Garden House.
- Square 24, House of the Heart: In the house of love and emotion, the Heart prompts a female player who just rolled the dice to advance to the Querent's square, square 28, to offer him her love. For a male player, he should advance to the female querent's square, square 29,

to offer his heart.

- Square 25, House of the Ring: Whoever reaches the golden ring receives three marks.
- Square 26, House of the Book: Anyone who opens the secret book is punished and sent to square 20, the Garden House.
- Square 27, House of the Letter: The visitor of the House of the Letter must pay two marks to the messenger to read it.
- Square 28, House of the Lady: The good lady, delighted by the visit of a male player, sends him to square 31, the Sun House. However, if he was sent here by the Heart, he will not receive the lady's bonus. A female player arriving at the lady's house receives no favor and must wait her turn to continue the game.
- Square 29, House of the Man: The gentleman of this house gallantly leads the female player to square 32, the Moon House. If she arrived via the Heart, she will not receive this bonus. A male player arriving at this square receives no favor and must wait his turn to continue the game.
- Square 33, House of the Key: Upon reaching the key to success, the player receives two marks.
- Square 34, House of the Fish: Upon reaching the House of Fish, the player must pay two marks.
- Square 35, House of the Anchor of Hope: If you arrive first, you win! You receive all the accumulated money and the prize pool.
- Square 36, House of the Cross: Another jail square; the only way to get free is for another player to roll doubles.

If a roll moves you past square 36, for example, if the player is on square 32 and rolls an 8, they advance four squares and then move back four more to reach a total of eight. So, they would land on square 28.

The Game of Hope serves as a foundational reference for many meanings within the Lenormand system, illustrating their origins. This method has also inspired the creation of modern divination tools, such as charm casting. In this practice, charms featuring Lenormand symbols are tossed onto a board, and the symbol's interpretation aligns with the meaning of the square where it lands. This approach creates an interactive divination experience, blending elements of cleromancy (the art of casting) with Lenormand and traditional board game mechanics.

German Traditional Lenormand Core Meanings

1. The Rider: News
2. The Clover: Small luck, joy
3. The Ship: Prosperous trade and mobility
4. The House: Favorable outcomes in your actions/surroundings
5. The Tree: Health and well-being
6. The Clouds: Trouble
7. The Snake: Betrayal
8. The Coffin: Death, illness, loss
9. The Bouquet: Happiness
10. The Scythe: Danger
11. The Whip: Discord
12. The Birds: Stress and annoyance
13. The Child: Ease
14. The Fox: Wrongness
15. The Bear: Fortune accompanied by covetousness
16. The Stars: Luck
17. The Stork: Change
18. The Dog: Loyalty
19. The Tower: Longevity
20. The Garden: Pleasant company
21. The Mountain: Enemy, obstacle
22. The Crossroads: Difficult choices
23. The Mice: Loss
24. The Heart: Well-being
25. The Ring: Union
26. The Book: The hidden
27. The Letter: Communication

28. The Man: Significant male figure, often the querent for women
29. The Woman: Significant female figure, often the querent for men
30. The Lily: Satisfaction and sexuality
31. The Sun: Luck and joy
32. The Moon: Honor
33. The Key: Success
34. The Fish: Prosperity
35. The Anchor: Successful transactions and wealth
36. The Cross: Grief

CHAPTER 5

Belgium and the Vincent Brepols Deck

Belgium is a remarkable country, celebrated not only for its stunning landscapes and rich history but also for its impressive multilingualism. The people here often speak three to four languages fluently, reflecting a cultural tapestry woven from diverse influences. In fact, many Belgians speak French with a level of proficiency that sometimes surpasses that of native French speakers! Their command of grammar is particularly impressive, showcasing a profound respect for language and communication. This linguistic diversity is also evident in their cultural practices, including a strong adherence to the traditional Lenormand system, likely influenced by their proximity to Germany.

My own journey into the world of Lenormand began with the Vincent Brepols deck (ca. 1901), which aligns with the meanings established by Philippe Lenormand that we discussed earlier.

Each card in this unique deck features the card number alongside its corresponding playing-card insert, complete with the French playing-card symbols. Additionally, you'll find a quatrain—a four-line poem—that encapsulates the card's meaning, serving as a helpful mnemonic for readers. This special deck was a gift from my uncle, who brought it back from his trip to Belgium. At the time, I had been eagerly hoping for a Tarot deck, anticipating the symbols and archetypes that Tarot provides. Instead, I was presented with this intriguing Lenormand deck. As they say, when life gives you lemons, you make lemonade! Little did I know that this unexpected gift would open the door to a fascinating exploration of divination and interpretation.

The full meanings provided in the Philippe Lenormand sheet not only guide readings but also enhance the reader's connection to the cards. In Belgium, Lenormand readings closely resemble those practiced in Germany. Most practitioners lay out the Grand Tableau in a similar manner, employing the Method of Distance and utilizing meanings derived from Philippe's interpretation sheet.

The Philippe Lenormand Sheet reads as follows:

1. Rider: The messenger of good fortune, indicating positive news when not surrounded by negative cards. If distant, it may relate to a person's residence or arrivals from foreign lands.
2. Clover: A harbinger of good news, but if surrounded by clouds, it forewarns of great pain. When near the querent, any sorrows will likely be short-lived and have a happy ending.
3. Ship: Symbolizing commerce, this card signifies great wealth acquired through trade or inheritance. If near the querent, it indicates a journey.
4. House: Represents success and prosperity in all undertakings. Even in unfortunate situations, a better future is anticipated. If located in the center of the spread, it suggests caution regarding those around the querent.
5. Tree: When distant from the querent, it signifies health. Multiple Tree cards indicate the fulfillment of wishes and a bright future.
6. Clouds: If the clear side faces the querent, it signifies a happy sign. However, if the dark side is visible, trouble may soon arise.
7. Snake: A sign of misfortune, its meaning varies on the basis of proximity to the querent. It often signifies deceit, infidelity, and sorrow.
8. Coffin: If very close to the querent, it indicates serious illness, death, or total loss of fortune. Its danger decreases as it moves farther away.
9. Bouquet: Represents much happiness in all aspects of life.
10. Scythe: An omen of great danger, which can be avoided only if surrounded by positive cards.
11. Rod: Indicates discord in the family, domestic sorrows, and possible illness.
12. Birds: Signifies difficulties that will be short-lived. When far from the querent, it suggests a happy trip.
13. Child: Symbolizes good associations and a generous nature toward others.
14. Fox: If close, this card warns to be cautious of those around you, since someone may seek to deceive. If distant, there is no cause for concern.

15. Bear: Can represent either good fortune or the need to distance oneself from envious company.
16. Star: Signifies success in all endeavors, but if near clouds, it warns of potential misfortunes.
17. Stork: Indicates a change of residence, with proximity to the querent suggesting a quicker transition.
18. Dog: Proximity ensures faithful friendships, but if distant and surrounded by clouds, it warns against trusting those who claim to be friends.
19. Tower: Signifies a long and happy life, but clouds nearby forewarn of illness or even death.
20. Garden: Indicates gatherings with respected company; if very close, it shows intimate friendships, while distance may suggest false friends.
21. Mountain: Proximity warns of a powerful enemy, but when distant, it suggests the presence of strong allies.
22. Crossroads: Surrounded by clouds, it signals misfortune; when distant from both the clouds and the querent, it suggests available means to escape danger.
23. Mouse: A sign of theft; if near, it implies recovery of the stolen item, but if far, the loss may be irretrievable.
24. Heart: Signifies joy, union, and bliss.
25. Ring: When to the right of the querent, it announces a rich and happy marriage; if removed and to the left, it suggests a broken engagement or separation.
26. Book: Indicates that a secret will come to light, and its position helps determine its significance. Caution is advised when uncovering it.
27. Letter: Without Clouds, it signifies happiness from pleasant news. If accompanied by Clouds, sorrow may follow.
28. Gentleman: Represents a significant male figure in the querent's life.
29. Lady: Represents a significant female figure in the querent's life.
30. Lily: Indicates a happy life, but surrounded by Clouds, it may point to family grief. Positioned above the querent, it signifies virtue; below, it raises doubts about their morals.

31. Sun: When close, it brings happiness and growth, but from a distance, it cools and suggests sorrow or misfortune. Without the Sun's influence, nothing can flourish.
32. Moon: Signifies great honor and fame when close; if distant, it foretells misfortune.
33. Key: Proximity indicates certain success in matters, while distance suggests the opposite.
34. Fish: Near the querent, it signifies success in maritime ventures and profitable endeavors. If distant, it warns of project failures, regardless of preparation.
35. Anchor: Represents luck in trade and love when close. When distant, it indicates errors in judgment and fleeting romantic interests.
36. Cross: Generally an unlucky card, but if very close, it may offer hope that the situation won't last long.

Notably, Mademoiselle Lenormand traveled to Belgium many times in her life. She went there in April 1821, with the intention of presenting her latest book to the king of the Netherlands, but was instead arrested on charges of witchcraft, likely influenced by the political claims in her book that were favorable to France.

During her time in France, Mademoiselle Lenormand made a significant impression, and her skills as a prolific cartomancer captivated many. As a result, French divination methods were adopted by the people of Belgium. Mademoiselle Lenormand is known for practicing the Grand Jeu, a method similar to the Grand Tableau, where all cards are used in a board formation. For her, this involved a picket deck of thirty-two cards, arranged into a tableau of four lines of eight cards each, with the significator based on the subject's sex, age, physique, color, and stature.

Occasionally, four cards would be set aside, referred to as "la surprise," which provided a final interpretation to the reading, revealing a more profound insight. This concept likely inspired the 8 × 4 + 4 Grand Tableau format, where the final four cards, called the "line of destiny," serve a purpose similar to "la surprise."

CHAPTER 6

France, Home to Mlle. Lenormand

France is globally renowned for its rich cultural, historical, and intellectual legacy. The country is known as the birthplace of haute cuisine, and French food and wine are celebrated worldwide, with regions such as Bordeaux and Burgundy producing some of the finest wines, and French dishes such as croissants, escargot, and coq au vin becoming culinary icons. Paris, often regarded as the fashion capital of the world, is home to luxury fashion houses such as Chanel, Dior, and Louis Vuitton, cementing France's place in the global fashion industry. The country's influence on art and philosophy is also profound, with masterpieces housed in the Louvre and thinkers such as Voltaire, Sartre, and Camus shaping Western thought. France's landmarks, including the Eiffel Tower and the Palace of Versailles, draw millions of visitors each year. Furthermore, France is synonymous with romance, and the melodious French language adds to the nation's charm. With prestigious institutions such as the Sorbonne, a storied film industry, and world-famous events such as the Tour de France and Cannes Film Festival, France continues to be a leader in arts, culture, and intellectualism.

But before France became known for its haute cuisine, fashion, and art, it had already earned a reputation as a center of mysticism and spiritualism. The country was home to some of the most famous psychic mediums, fortune-tellers, and card readers of the eighteenth and nineteenth centuries, who captivated the French elite with their abilities. One of the earliest pioneers of cartomancy, Jean-Baptiste Alliette, better known simply as Etteilla, revolutionized fortune-telling through Tarot cards, creating one of the first Tarot decks specifically designed for divination. Others, such as Marie-Anne Lenormand and Eugène Caslant, rose to prominence, blending esoteric traditions with elements of the occult and leaving an enduring legacy that continues to influence modern spiritual practices. France, with its deep connection to mysticism, became a hub for psychic activity, where famous readers were consulted by politicians, aristocrats, and even royalty.

Mlle. Lenormand stands out as perhaps the most legendary and influential cartomancer of all. Marie-Anne Lenormand, born on May 27, 1772, in Alençon, Orne, came from a merchant family. Her early education took place at the Benedictine convent, where she demonstrated a natural talent for languages, music, and arts. By the time she was eight, her ability to predict the future already intrigued her peers. This early intuition would shape her path toward becoming one of Europe's most renowned fortune-tellers.

Orphaned and without financial support, Lenormand first worked as a seamstress apprentice before transitioning to a cashier role in a lingerie shop. Drawn to Paris just before the French Revolution, she found employment in the textile trade and later became a reader for Count d'Amerval de la Saussotte. In 1789, she began making predictions that aligned with the political turmoil, accurately foreseeing shifts within the clergy and the closure of convents.

In 1790, she traveled to London to consult Dr. Gall, a famed phrenologist, who confirmed her gift of divination. Upon returning to Paris, Lenormand's destiny was shaped by two key individuals: Louise Françoise Gilbert, who taught her the art of cartomancy, and Flammermont, a baker's assistant. Together, they opened a business in the bustling Rue de Tournon, where Lenormand established her fortune-telling practice under the guise of a "young American" offering unique talents to the French.

Her rise to fame was swift. Lenormand quickly became the go-to fortune-teller for political figures, including Robespierre, Danton, and Desmoulin, reading their futures through Tarot cards and coffee grounds. She ran her practice in a modest ground-floor apartment, where anxious clients waited in the salon while her assistant, now posing as an usher, led them into her sanctuary. Her consultations were tailored to the clients' budgets, ranging from ten to eighty francs, and included psychological assessments based on detailed personal questions.

Lenormand's success was not without challenges. In 1793, Robespierre had her arrested after she predicted a counterrevolution. Imprisoned at La Petite Force, she consoled noblewomen, promising them future freedom. During her time there, Lenormand's predictions caught the attention of a young prisoner named Marie-Rose de Beauharnais, later known as Empress Josephine. Lenormand foresaw the death of Josephine's first husband, General Beauharnais, and predicted her second marriage to a young officer destined for greatness—none other than Napoleon Bonaparte. This forecast cemented Josephine's loyalty to Lenormand for years to come.

After her release in 1794, Lenormand's clientele grew to include prominent figures such as Barras, Tallien, and the famed actress Juliette Récamier. She became a fixture of Parisian society during the Directory, Consulate, and Empire, reading for military officers, artists, and socialites. Her methods expanded beyond Tarot and coffee grounds, scrying with crystal, water, and candle flames, and even melted lead to divine the future.

Though her popularity continued to soar, Lenormand's relationship with Empress Josephine put her in a precarious position with Napoleon. The emperor, wary of her influence over his wife, had her arrested in 1803 after she predicted the arrest of General Moreau and prophesied the failure of an English invasion. Though briefly imprisoned, she was freed, possibly through Josephine's intervention, and resumed her work under the watchful eyes of Napoleon's secret police.

Despite the political tension surrounding her predictions, Lenormand continued to thrive. She attracted high-profile clients such as the Persian ambassador and Mme. Junot, all eager to hear her insights. As Napoleon's power grew, so did his unease with Lenormand's prophecies. In 1808, Josephine repeated Lenormand's warning about his policies toward Rome, further straining their relationship. Napoleon ridiculed Josephine for consulting the fortune-teller but recognized the political utility of her insights.

In December 1809, during the turbulent period of the imperial divorce, Lenormand was once again arrested. Accused of earning vast sums from her predictions, she remained undeterred, confronting Fouché, the minister of police, with bold prophecies about his downfall. Though imprisoned several times, she always managed to secure her release, often through her connections with influential figures. Marie-Anne Lenormand's life was a testament to her extraordinary abilities, both as a fortune-teller and a keen observer of human nature. Despite the political unrest and personal dangers she faced, she left an indelible mark on the world of divination, forever remembered as the most famous sibyl of her time.

After the death of Marie-Anne Lenormand in 1843, her fame only seemed to grow. Her influence had become so widespread that many illegitimate and opportunistic people claimed to be her apprentices or protégés. As her fame expanded, everyone seemed eager to lay claim to some part of her legacy. The reputation of Mademoiselle Lenormand was such that even after her death, association with her name carried prestige. Cartomancers began to adapt and reinterpret her methods, often adding their own innovations and, in some cases, falsely attributing their work to her teachings.

It was during this period that the Lenormand deck we know today began to take shape. Various individuals capitalized on her fame, rebrand-

The grave of Mademoiselle Lenormand at Père Lachaise cemetery in the Third Division, Paris, France. (If you want to visit her, a video providing full directions from the metro line in Paris is available on my YouTube channel.)

ing existing decks or creating entirely new ones under her name to boost their credibility. This is where the creator of the Petit Lenormand decided to immortalize her legacy by publishing a unique thirty-six-card deck, aligning it with the teachings that were often associated with Lenormand herself. The deck was simpler than the Grand Jeu but still contained rich symbolic imagery that appealed to the public. It became incredibly popular, and today the Petit Lenormand is used by readers around the world, further cementing Mademoiselle Lenormand's lasting impact on the art of cartomancy.

Mademoiselle Lenormand is buried in the historic Père Lachaise Cemetery in Paris, a fitting resting place for a woman whose life and work left an indelible mark on the world of cartomancy and divination. Her legacy continues to resonate, drawing visitors and admirers to her final resting place, where they pay homage to a true pioneer of the art.

French Cartomancy: The Tradition of the Piquet Deck and Its Evolution

French cartomancy has a long and storied history, rooted in the use of playing cards as tools for divination. One of the most traditional decks used in French cartomancy is the Piquet deck, a deck of thirty-two cards consisting of only the ranks from 7 through ace in the four standard suits: hearts, diamonds, clubs, and spades. The origins of this deck date back to the seventeenth century, and it was originally used for the popular French card game Piquet. However, over time, cartomancers adapted this deck for fortune-telling, assigning meanings to each card on the basis of its suit and rank.

The Structure of the Piquet Deck

The Piquet deck, unlike a standard deck of fifty-two cards, omits the 2s through 6s. It contains the following ranks in each suit:

- 7, 8, 9, 10, jack, queen, king, ace
- In French cartomancy, each suit is associated with different aspects of life:
- Hearts represent emotions, love, and relationships.
- Diamonds are linked to money, material possessions, and communication.
- Clubs typically signify challenges, work, and effort.
- Spades are associated with obstacles, conflict, and sorrow in the French system.

The Lenormand deck also includes playing-card inserts derived from the Piquet deck. However, it's important to note that the Lenormand system is of German origin, and the meanings of the suits and cards differ greatly from the French tradition.

For instance, in the German system, spades are considered positive cards, which is contrary to their French interpretation. On the other hand, clubs are seen as the cards of difficulty and negativity in German cartomancy, making the two systems quite distinct. This is why many of the negative cards in the Lenormand deck correspond to clubs, exception for the Bear (10 of Clubs) and the Ring (Ace of Clubs).

Below is a comparison of the playing cards found in the Lenormand deck and their traditional meanings in both German and French cartomancy systems.

Hearts

Card	Lenormand Meaning (German Influence)	French Cartomancy Meaning
6 of Hearts	Stars: Success, guidance, inspiration	Memories, hope
7 of Hearts	Tree: Health, longevity, personal growth	Tranquility, positive feelings, can sometimes represent a child
8 of Hearts	Moon: Recognition, intuition, dreams	A young girl, sensitive person, a good heart, a sister
9 of Hearts	Rider: News, new beginnings, movement	Positive outcome, a victory, a wish come true
10 of Hearts	Dog: Loyalty, friendship, trust	Positive issue, an invitation, a celebration
Jack of Hearts	Heart: Love, affection, deep emotions	Young blond man, idealistic, great sensitivity, a lover, a fiancé, a brother
Queen of Hearts	Stork: Change, transformation, progress	Beloved, a mother, fair skin, female querent
King of Hearts	House: Stability, family, home	A protector, a good man, devoted person, male querent
Ace of Hearts	Letter: Communication, message, important news	Personal life, joy, pleasure, falling in love, the home

Diamonds

Card	Lenormand Meaning (German Influence)	French Cartomancy Meaning
6 of Diamonds	Clover: Luck, opportunity, happiness	Reward, small gift, surprise
7 of Diamonds	Birds: Communication, gossip, conversations	Projects, plans, transaction
8 of Diamonds	Key: Destiny, important discoveries, solutions	A confirmation, a target, a goal
9 of Diamonds	Coffin: Endings, transformation, illness	Blockage, delays, standstill
10 of Diamonds	Fish: Abundance, wealth, business	Travel, change, movement, relocation
Jack of Diamonds	Child: Innocence, new beginnings, simplicity	Message bearer, news, decision, ex-lover
Queen of Diamonds	Crossroads: Decisions, choices, alternative paths	Jealousy, a rival, a warning, a foreigner, gossip, ex-wife
King of Diamonds	Sun: Success, positivity, energy	a businessman, a foreigner, ambitious man, ex-husband
Ace of Diamonds	Fox: Deception, strategy, cunning	News, information, letter, contract

Spades

Card	Lenormand Meaning (German Influence)	French Cartomancy Meaning
6 of Spades	Mountain: Obstacles, delays, challenges	Argument, discussion, small trouble
7 of Spades	Clouds: Confusion, uncertainty, problems	Certifies an event, favorable event, for sure, a yes answer
8 of Spades	Garden: Social activities, community, networking	Feeling tired, drained, exhausted; health issue
9 of Spades	Anchor: Stability, perseverance, career	Unexpected event, fatality, danger
10 of Spades	Ship: Travel, adventure, business	Very quick, doubts, by night
Jack of Spades	Whip: Conflict, arguments, strife	Warning, betrayal, childish, a traitor
Queen of Spades	Snake: Deception, betrayal, complications	A widow, divorced woman, mature woman, grandmother
King of Spades	Lily: Purity, virtue, peace	A widower, divorced man, mature man, grandfather
Ace of Spades	Woman: Feminine energy, woman in the querent's life	An opening, legal papers, separation

Clubs

Card	Lenormand Meaning (German Influence)	French Cartomancy Meaning
6 of Clubs	Tower: Authority, isolation, boundaries	Obstacles, pain, difficulties
7 of Clubs	Mice: Loss, stress, anxiety	Thoughts, your hope, your expectations
8 of Clubs	Bear: Power, strength, protection	A brunette, small sum of money, nephew, cousin
9 of Clubs	Ring: Commitment, contracts, partnership	Your work, your day job, what pays the bills
10 of Clubs	Cross: Burden, suffering, hardship	Abundance, prosperity, large sum of money
Jack of Clubs	Man: Masculine energy, man in the querent's life	Young man, attracted by money, nephew, cousin
Queen of Clubs	Bouquet: Gifts, beauty, charm	A mature woman, close to her money, an aunt
King of Clubs	Tree: Health, personal growth, family heritage	A mature man, close to his money, an uncle
Ace of Clubs	Letter: Communication, important news, messages	Triumph, great success, alliance

As the table demonstrates, although Lenormand uses the same Piquet deck playing-card inserts, their meanings in German cartomancy are often vastly different from their interpretations in French cartomancy. French tradition, with its roots in challenges and obstacles reflected in the suit of spades, contrasts with German cartomancy, where spades are more favorable and clubs take on the more negative role. This is why in France, the fox is the job card and the bear is the money card.

Below is a rearranged list of Lenormand cards aligned to the French classic cartomancy meanings, with the correct playing-card inserts placed alongside the corresponding Lenormand symbols. This list will help you understand how traditional French cartomancers modified the card meaning in relation to Philippe Lenormand interpretations.

Lenormand Cards	Aligned to the Classic French Cartomancy
Rider	Jack of Diamonds
Clover	8 of Clubs
Ship	10 of Diamonds
House	Ace of Hearts
Tree	8 of Spades
Clouds	7 of Clubs
Snake	Queen of Diamonds
Coffin	Ace of Spades
Bouquet	8 of Hearts
Scythe	10 of Spades
Whip	6 of Spades
Birds	6 of Diamonds
Child	7 of Hearts
Fox	9 of Clubs
Bear	10 of Clubs
Stars	6 of Hearts
Stork	Queen of Hearts
Dog	King of Hearts

(continued)

Lenormand Cards	Aligned to the Classic French Cartomancy
Tower	Queen of Diamonds
Garden	10 of Hearts
Mountain	9 of Diamonds
Crossroads	7 of Diamonds
Mice	Jack of Spades
Heart	Jack of Hearts
Ring	7 of Spades
Book	Jack of Clubs
Letter	Ace of Diamonds
Man	King of Clubs
Woman	Queen of Clubs
Lily	King of Spades
Sun	Ace of Clubs
Moon	10 of Spades
Key	9 of Hearts
Fish	King of Diamonds
Anchor	8 of Diamonds
Cross	6 of Clubs

CHAPTER 7

From France to l'île Bourbon

L'île Bourbon, now known as Réunion Island, holds a deep and complex history that reflects centuries of colonization, cultural blending, and resilience in the face of adversity. This small volcanic island in the Indian Ocean, once a French colony and now a French department (in some ways like Hawaii and Puerto Rico to the US in terms of their political status as territories or integral parts of larger countries), is a land shaped by its people, many of whom were brought against their will. Their traditions, beliefs, and survival strategies created the rich spiritual and cultural heritage that defines the island today.

Réunion Island, formerly called l'île Bourbon, was first charted by European explorers in the early sixteenth century but remained largely uninhabited until the mid-1600s. The French took interest in the island for its strategic location along the trade routes between Europe, India, and Southeast Asia, and by 1642 the French East India Company claimed the island. The settlers began arriving in 1665, laying the foundation for the colony that would later become a thriving center for agricultural production. As the colony grew, so did the demand for labor. Sugarcane, introduced in the eighteenth century, quickly became the primary crop, and with it came the need for intensive labor. Unable to meet these demands with European settlers alone, the French began importing enslaved Africans and Malagasy from nearby Madagascar and mainland Africa. Slaves arrived on the island in chains, deprived of their freedom and dignity and often stripped of their identities. They were brought to cultivate the sugarcane fields, which soon became the backbone of the island's economy. These men, women, and children had no belongings and no connection to the land and were treated as property. The masters forced them to labor under brutal conditions, often working from sunrise to sunset. But the enslaved Africans brought with them something invaluable—an indomitable spirit and the rich traditions of their ancestors. Their languages, spiritual practices, and healing knowledge traveled with them across the seas. However, under the eyes of the colonial masters, these spiritual practices were labeled as "witchcraft," and the enslaved people were forced to abandon them. Catholicism was imposed on the population as part of the colonial system's efforts to "civilize" the enslaved people, with the church acting as a tool of control. The masters wanted to erase the slaves' traditions, and the church encouraged conversion to Catholicism, demanding that they renounce their gods and beliefs.

Despite these oppressive efforts, the enslaved people found ways to preserve their spiritual identities. Although they were forced to attend mass and outwardly adopt the practices of the Catholic Church, many of them cleverly hid their true beliefs under the guise of Catholicism. On the same altars where the Virgin Mary, Saint Anthony, and Jesus were worshiped, they quietly honored their ancestors and spirits. This syncretic blending of African, Malagasy, and Catholic beliefs allowed them to disguise their traditional practices under the appearance of Christian worship. For instance,

saints such as Mary and Jesus were often seen as spiritual proxies for African deities and ancestral spirits. In the eyes of the colonial masters, they were good Catholics, but behind the scenes, they were honoring the gods of their ancestors and keeping their traditions alive. This hidden resistance was an act of spiritual defiance, an ingenious way to protect their sacred beliefs from being completely erased.

This syncretic spirituality became the foundation of Creole magick, which blends African, Malagasy, and European spiritual influences. Even today, you can see the traces of this cultural survival in the island's practices of veneration, with altars often displaying Catholic imagery alongside offerings to ancestors and spirits from Africa and Madagascar.

The abolition of slavery in 1848 marked a turning point in the history of Réunion Island. However, the end of slavery did not mean the end of the plantation system. Freed from the chains of slavery, many of the formerly enslaved people sought out new opportunities, but the landowners still needed labor to maintain the island's thriving sugar industry. To replace the freed labor force, the French began bringing in indentured laborers, primarily from India and China. Unlike the enslaved Africans and Malagasy who had arrived before them, these workers came under a formal contract. They were not chained, and they had some basic rights. Perhaps most importantly, they were allowed to bring their belongings with them. These belongings included not only personal items but also the seeds of their cultural and spiritual traditions. The Indian and Chinese laborers arrived with plants, spices, and representations of their deities—Shivji, Kalima, Lakshmi Mata, Buddhist figures—which they openly worshiped in their homes. This arrival of indentured workers brought new layers to the island's spiritual and cultural fabric. Hinduism and Chinese traditions blended with the preexisting African and Malagasy beliefs. Over time, these diverse practices merged into a distinctly Creole spiritual identity, which continues to thrive on the island today. The Indian laborers, in particular, contributed immensely to the formation of Creole magick by integrating their knowledge of plants, spices, and rituals, further enriching the island's spiritual practices.

The blending of African, Malagasy, Indian, Chinese, and European influences created something unique in the Indian Ocean: Creole magick. This spiritual practice draws on the ancestral knowledge of many cultures and reflects the island's deep history of cultural fusion. Creole magick uses plants, herbs, spices, and prayers from diverse traditions, blending Catholic prayers with invocations to African spirits or Hindu gods. Even though the enslaved Africans were denied the right to openly honor their gods, their traditions persisted in secret and eventually merged with the practices brought by the indentured laborers. Catholic saints stand beside representations of African spirits and Indian deities, all part of a larger spiritual framework that reflects the island's history of oppression, survival, and cultural blending.

Creole magick is not just a spiritual practice; it is a testament to the resilience of the people of Réunion, and I am living proof of that powerful legacy of art and spirituality. My own lineage reflects the rich diversity that characterizes this island. On my father's side, my ancestors came from India, bringing with them the sacred traditions, deities, and spiritual practices that have woven their way into the fabric of Creole life. On my mother's side, European and African ancestry combined to create a unique *métissage*—a blend of cultures that mirrors the island's own history.

This heritage has given me an intimate connection to the spiritual pathways that took root in the soil of Réunion, where, even in the darkest times, enslaved people, laborers, and their descendants held fast to their roots. Despite the brutal forces that tried to strip them of their identity, they maintained their connection to their ancestors and their gods, sometimes in secret, sometimes under the cloak of Catholicism, but always with an unyielding spirit.

When the French settlers arrived on the island, their suitcases didn't just carry clothes, rosaries, or Bibles. They also brought with them items that would keep them entertained in this wild, forested land, and one of those items was a deck of playing cards. Alongside their religious and practical belongings, the French introduced their traditions, including the art of reading cards. In their homes, ladies of the household would secretly read cards, making predictions about love, marriage, and other daily affairs. The cards were more than just a game—they were a tool to foresee the future.

The slaves, who worked as servants in these households, witnessed these card readings firsthand. Those among them who had the gift of sight recognized the cards as a new form of a familiar practice. In their homeland, their ancestors had used bones, shells, and other objects to divine the future. Though they saw the potential of the cards as a divinatory tool, they were not allowed to possess or use them. As always, the slaves adapted. They learned in silence, carefully observing the practices of their masters. Through whispered conversations and word of mouth, the knowledge of reading cards passed from one spiritual individual to the next.

It wasn't until after the abolition of slavery that the now-free people could use the cards, but still in secret. They integrated this practice into their own spiritual traditions, adding another layer to their complex spiritual landscape. Today, this practice still thrives. Playing cards and their divinatory meanings became part of Creole spirituality, syncretized with ancestral beliefs.

CHAPTER 8

Divine Guidance

I started reading playing cards as a young boy, learning from my family's legacy while adapting the practice to fit the modern world. Over time, I was introduced to the Lenormand deck, and much like what happened in France, we on the island mixed the traditional Lenormand with our own form of cartomancy. However, we added our own twist by syncretizing the Lenormand cards with our saints, spirits, and ancestors.

For instance, in our readings, Lord Shiva is symbolized by the combination of the Snake and the Mountain cards—the snake representing the serpent or cobra that coils around Shiva's neck, and the mountain standing for Mount Kailasa, Shiva's sacred abode. The Lilies and the Bouquet, meanwhile, came to represent the Holy Virgin Mary and Saint Joseph. Another example is the Whip card combined with the Cross card, which in our tradition represents Saint Expedite, the patron saint of the island.

In this way, just as the French colonists had once done, we have made the cards our own, weaving them into the fabric of our spiritual and cultural heritage. What started as a tool of entertainment and fortune-telling has become, in our hands, a sacred method of connecting with the divine, the ancestors, and the spirits that guide us.

Here's a list for each Lenormand card, with examples of corresponding Catholic saints and Hindu deities. The interpretations blend traditional meanings of the Lenormand symbols with figures from Catholicism and Hinduism, reflecting a syncretic approach that mirrors how spiritual traditions on Réunion Island adapted these symbols.

1. Rider (Cavalier)

Catholic saint: Saint Christopher, the patron saint of travelers, associated with movement and new messages

Hindu deity: Hanuman, the god known for swift action and carrying important messages, much like the Rider

2. Clover (Trèfle)

Catholic saint: Saint Benedict, known for his powerful protection against negative energies. His sacred medal is used as a talisman for protection.

Hindu deity: Lakshmi, goddess of wealth and fortune, blessing those with prosperity

3. Ship (Navire)

Catholic saint: Saint Brendan, patron saint of sailors and voyagers, often linked with travel and exploration

Hindu deity: Varuna, god of the oceans and seas, protector of travelers on water

4. House (Maison)

Catholic saint: Saint Joseph, patron saint of homes and families, symbolizing protection and domestic harmony

Hindu deity: Vastu Purusha, the deity associated with the construction of homes and maintaining harmony within them

5. Tree (Arbre)

Catholic saint: Saint Raphael, the healing angel, connected with health and well-being, much like the Tree card

Hindu deity: Dhanvantari, the god of medicine and healing, representing vitality and growth

6. Clouds (Nuages)

Catholic saint: Saint Jude, patron saint of lost causes, associated with uncertainty and confusion but also with hope

Hindu deity: Indra, god of storms and rain, symbolizing both power and the chaos of clouds

7. Snake (Serpent)

Catholic saint: Saint Patrick, known for driving snakes out of Ireland, a symbol of overcoming deceit or challenges

Hindu deity: Shiva, often depicted with a snake around his neck, representing both danger and spiritual transformation

8. Coffin (Cercueil)

Catholic saint: Saint Lazarus, symbolizing resurrection and overcoming death. The Coffin also represents the souls in purgatory, who are in a state of spiritual purification.

Hindu deity: Yama, god of death, associated with transformation and the cycle of life and death

9. Bouquet

Catholic saint: Saint Thérèse of Lisieux, known for her "Little Way" and the symbolic offering of flowers, connected to beauty and grace

Hindu deity: Saraswati, goddess of art, beauty, and wisdom, often depicted holding flowers or a garland

10. Scythe (Faux)

Catholic saint: Saint Michael, the archangel known for his sword, symbolizing cutting away evil or unnecessary things

Hindu deity: Kali, goddess of destruction, who cuts away illusion and negativity

11. Whip (Fouet)

Catholic saint: Saint Expedite, known for quick resolutions and petitions, associated with urgency and discipline

Hindu deity: Durga, warrior goddess who fights evil, symbolizing justice and swift action

12. Birds (Oiseaux)

Catholic saint: Saint Francis of Assisi, known for his love of animals and nature, symbolizing communication and connection

Hindu deity: Garuda, the divine eagle, a messenger of the gods, symbolizing communication and freedom

13. Child (Enfant)

Catholic saint: Infant Jesus of Prague, symbolizing innocence and new beginnings

Hindu deity: Ganesha, the childlike deity who removes obstacles, associated with fresh starts and new ventures

14. Fox (Renard)

Catholic saint: Saint Martin of Tours, associated with protection and cleverness in difficult situations

Hindu deity: Vishnu (in his Krishna avatar), known for his cleverness and ability to navigate difficult situations

15. Bear (Ours)

Catholic saint: Saint Brigid, associated with strength, protection, and nurturing

Hindu deity: Durga, the powerful goddess who rides a lion, representing strength and maternal protection

16. Stars (Étoiles)

Catholic saint: Saint Dominic, founder of the Rosary, symbolizing guidance, prayer, and heavenly connection

Hindu deity: Agni, god of fire and stars, symbolizing divine light and guidance

17. Stork (Cigogne)

Catholic saint: Saint Anne, the mother of Mary, symbolizing family and transitions

Hindu deity: Parvati, goddess of motherhood and transformation

18. Dog (Chien)

Catholic saint: Saint Roch, the patron saint of dogs and loyalty, symbolizing friendship and devotion. Saint Joseph, guardian of the Holy Family.

Hindu deity: Bhairava, a form of Shiva often accompanied by a dog, representing loyalty and protection

19. Tower (Tour)

Catholic saint: Saint Barbara, the patron saint of those who work in towers or are in danger of lightning strikes, symbolizing protection and boundaries

Hindu deity: Brahma, god of creation, often associated with order and structure

20. Garden (Jardin)

Catholic saint: Saint Fiacre, the patron saint of gardeners, symbolizing community and cultivation

Hindu deity: Krishna, often associated with pastoral scenes and gardens, representing joy and harmony

21. Mountain (Montagne)

Catholic saint: Saint Bernard, the patron saint of mountaineers and those traveling in treacherous conditions, representing obstacles

Hindu deity: Shiva, residing on Mount Kailasa, symbolizing spiritual challenge and endurance

22. Crossroads (Chemins)

Catholic saint: Saint Christopher, a guide at life's crossroads, helping people make decisions

Hindu deity: Ganesha, remover of obstacles, associated with making choices and new paths

23. Mice (Souris)

Catholic saint: Saint Anthony of Padua, associated with miracles and blessings. Patron saint of lost objects, lost people, and lost causes.

Hindu deity: Ganesha, whose *vahana* (vehicle) is a mouse, symbolizing the removal of negative influences

24. Heart (Cœur)

Catholic saint: Sacred Heart of Jesus, symbolizing love, compassion, and devotion

Hindu deity: Radha, goddess of love and devotion, symbolizing passion and connection

25. Ring (Anneau)

Catholic saint: Saint Valentine, patron saint of marriage and love, symbolizing commitment

Hindu deity: Parvati, goddess of marriage, love, and devotion

26. Book (Livre)

Catholic saint: Saint Jerome, patron saint of librarians and scholars, symbolizing knowledge and secrets

Hindu deity: Saraswati, goddess of knowledge and wisdom, often depicted with books

27. Letter (Lettre)

Catholic saint: Saint Gabriel, the archangel messenger, symbolizing communication and news

Hindu deity: Narada, the divine messenger and communicator, symbolizing divine news and wisdom

28. Man (Homme)

None: Since it represents the male querent

29. Woman (Femme)

None: Since it represents the female querent

30. Lilies (Lys)

Catholic saint: Saint Joseph, symbolizing purity, family, and peace

Hindu deity: Saraswati, goddess of purity and knowledge

31. Sun (Soleil)

Catholic saint: Saint John the Baptist, often associated with light and renewal. The Sun card reflects the supreme source of illumination—God himself.

Hindu deity: Surya, the sun god, representing energy and enlightenment

32. Moon (Lune)

Catholic saint: Saint Clare of Assisi, associated with the moon and its reflective light, symbolizing intuition and reflection

Hindu deity: Chandra, the moon god, symbolizing emotions, intuition, and cycles

33. Key (Clef)

Catholic saint: Saint Peter, traditionally depicted holding the keys to Heaven, symbolizing access, solutions, and important discoveries

Hindu deity: Ganesha, the remover of obstacles, representing the key to success and breakthroughs in difficult situations

34. Fish (Poisson)

Catholic saint: Saint Andrew, patron saint of fishermen, representing abundance, trade, and prosperity

Hindu deity: Lakshmi, goddess of wealth and fortune, blessing those with prosperity

35. Anchor (Ancre)

Catholic saint: Saint Nicholas, patron saint of sailors, symbolizing stability, hope, and perseverance

Hindu deity: Varuna, god of the sea, associated with security, stability, and enduring faith

36. Cross (Croix)

Catholic saint: Jesus Christ, the ultimate symbol of sacrifice, faith, and spiritual burdens. Saint Expedite, the holy martyr.

Hindu deity: Kali, representing the acceptance of fate and the endurance of life's struggles through spiritual strength

How to Use the Syncretized Method in a Reading

When integrating the spiritual meanings of saints and deities into a Lenormand reading, it's essential to understand that these meanings are used only in specific types of readings—particularly spiritual readings. A spiritual reading is distinct from a traditional Lenormand reading in that it seeks guidance directly from the spiritual realm. This kind of reading is not about predicting future events in the usual sense but, rather, about seeking advice, strategies, or solutions from higher powers, such as saints, gods, goddesses, or ancestral spirits.

The spiritual layer of interpretation that I have presented here offers a rich and profound way to engage with the Lenormand cards. Each card is connected with a saint or deity, giving you access to spiritual insights that go beyond the card's typical cartomantic meanings. However, it is important to understand that mastering this approach requires not only familiarity with the cards but also spiritual knowledge and, in many cases, a form of initiation.

Shifting the Focus: Core Meanings Become Secondary

When conducting a spiritual reading, the traditional meanings of the Lenormand cards, as per the Philippe Lenormand interpretations, take on a more secondary role. Normally, Lenormand cards are read with attention to their core meanings and polarity—whether the card is positive, negative, or neutral. However, in a spiritual reading, these classifications fade into the background. The focus shifts from the mundane to the sacred, allowing for deeper spiritual messages to emerge. For example:

- In a regular reading, the Snake card might indicate betrayal or complications. But in a spiritual reading, if connected with Lord Shiva, it could represent transformation, the shedding of old skin to reveal a new spiritual path, or divine wisdom.
- The Cross in a normal reading might indicate burdens or suffering, but in a spiritual context, especially when associated with Kali, it could speak of divine protection through difficult times, as well as the necessity of embracing life's challenges for spiritual growth.

The spiritual layer transcends the card's mundane interpretation, opening a space for spirit to communicate through symbols, saints, and deities that resonate on a higher plane. A spiritual reading requires a different approach in interpreting the cards. While the method of laying out the cards may remain the same, the meanings shift toward understanding divine intervention, guidance, and strategy provided by the spirit world.

In this case, you could draw a spread with the intention of asking for help from the spirits, saints, or gods connected to each card. For example, if you're struggling with a decision in life, you might ask for guidance from the divine and see which cards appear in the spread. Instead of focusing on whether the cards are traditionally positive or negative, you'll focus on the spiritual messages they contain, on the basis of their connection to saints or deities.

Three-Card Spiritual Spread

Lay three cards with the intention of seeking spiritual guidance. For example:

Card 1: What the spirits want you to know now
Card 2: The spiritual challenge or lesson
Card 3: The guidance or strategy provided by the spirits to overcome the challenge

In this spread, focus on the saint or deity associated with each card and what their influence suggests about your situation. Their messages will help you discern the spiritual steps you should take in response to your question.

Here is a sample reading that will help you see how a spiritual reading can be done safely.

SAMPLE READING: ISABELLE

Isabelle is a thirty-eight-year-old woman living on Réunion Island. She has recently gone through a difficult time with her family, experiencing tension and unresolved conflicts that have left her feeling disconnected and emotionally drained. She seeks spiritual guidance on how to heal these relationships and bring harmony back into her life. She believes that there is a deeper spiritual lesson she needs to learn from this situation, and wants to know how her ancestors and the divine can help her move forward.

Question: "How can I heal the rift within my family and restore peace, while also understanding the spiritual lesson behind this struggle?"

Card 1: What the spirits want you to know now: The Dog (card 18)

Saint/deity: Saint Joseph
Message from Spirit: Loyalty, protection, and trust
Interpretation: The spirits are reminding Isabelle of the importance of loyalty and trust within her relationships. Saint Joseph, known for his protective and fatherly role, suggests that the foundation of her family conflicts may be rooted in the need for security and reliability. The Dog card signifies that her ancestors are urging her to restore trust within her family, and they emphasize that true healing will come from showing loyalty and forgiveness, even when it's difficult. The spirits are with her, ready to offer protection as she navigates these emotional waters. Isabelle needs to focus on building bridges rather than letting her heart be weighed down by past hurts.

Card 2: The Spiritual Challenge or Lesson: The Clouds (King of Clubs)

Saint/deity: Saint Jude
Message from Spirit: Uncertainty, confusion, transformation
Interpretation: The Clouds card, aligned with Saint Jude, the patron saint of desperate and challenging situations, reflects the inner turmoil and uncertainty that Isabelle is experiencing. Saint Jude is guiding her through this period of confusion, reminding her that what seems like a hopeless situation is actually an opportunity for profound spiritual transformation. The tensions in her family are not just surface-level conflicts, but signs that deeper emotional shifts are taking place. Isabelle is being called to release old habits, grievances, and expectations that no longer serve her. This chaotic phase is a necessary step in her spiritual evolution, clearing the way for a new and more healthful family dynamic to emerge. The conflicts she faces externally are a mirror of the spiritual changes happening within, and embracing this transformation will allow her to move forward with renewed clarity and strength.

Card 3: The Guidance or Strategy Provided by the Spirits to Overcome the Challenge: The Bouquet (Queen of Spades)

Saint/deity: Sainte Thérèse of Lisieux
Message from Spirit: Grace, forgiveness, and blessings
Interpretation: The Bouquet card, aligned with Sainte Thérèse of Lisieux, conveys a profound message of grace and peace. The spirits are guiding Isabelle toward a path of forgiveness and compassion. Sainte Thérèse, known for her gentle spirit and "little way" of love, embodies nurturing and unconditional care. Isabelle is encouraged to open her heart in forgiveness—not just toward her family but also toward herself. The Bouquet signifies that as Isabelle embraces this loving energy, blessings will begin to flow back into her life. This healing process will foster harmony, both in her family relationships and within her own spirit. The spirits remind her that love and peace will ultimately triumph over any bitterness or hurt. By channeling the grace of Sainte Thérèse, Isabelle can cultivate an environment of understanding and compassion, setting the stage for lasting healing and connection.

In this reading, Isabelle is guided by the Divine to heal the rift within her family through loyalty, transformation, and forgiveness. The Dog card, associated with Saint Joseph, encourages her to stay devoted to her family, reminding her that trust is the foundation of healing. Rebuilding this trust will bring stability back into her relationships. The Clouds card, connected with Saint Jude, reveals that the current confusion and uncertainty are part of a larger spiritual challenge. Saint Jude, the patron saint of lost causes, shows that while the situation may seem overwhelming, Isabelle must have faith in divine intervention. This period of difficulty is an opportunity for transformation, and through prayer and persistence, she will find clarity and hope. The Bouquet card, linked to Saint Thérèse of Lisieux, carries a message of grace, peace, and forgiveness. Saint Thérèse, known for her "little way" of love and humility, guides Isabelle to embrace compassion for herself and her family. The Bouquet signifies that blessings will bloom in her life if she opens her heart to forgiveness and kindness.

Card 3 often suggests what spiritual practice can be done to improve the situation, and Saint Thérèse offers several pathways to peace. Isabelle is encouraged to work with Saint Thérèse by praying a novena dedicated to her, offering flowers as a symbol of love and purity, or taking a spiritual flower bath. This ritual will help cleanse her energy, invite peace and tranquility to blossom in her life, and restore harmony within her family.

By following this spiritual guidance and working with the saint, Isabelle can heal both her heart and her family relationships, inviting divine grace and blessings into her life.

SAMPLE READING: JULIEN

Julien is at a crossroads in his career and personal life. He feels the need for clarity regarding his path forward, especially concerning his family obligations and professional aspirations.

Question: "What guidance do the spirits have for me to find balance and direction in my life?"

Card 1: The Present Situation: Lilies (card 30)

Saint/deity: Saint Joseph, Saraswati
Message from Spirit: Purity, family, and knowledge
Interpretation: The Lilies card signifies a focus on family and inner peace in Julien's current situation. Saint Joseph represents a strong foundation of family values, urging Julien to prioritize his loved ones and cultivate a nurturing environment. Meanwhile, Saraswati, the goddess of knowledge and purity, encourages him to seek wisdom in his decisions. This card suggests that by embracing family values and pursuing knowledge, Julien can create a serene atmosphere that fosters personal growth and harmony.

Card 2: The Challenge to Overcome: Anchor (card 35)

Saint/deity: Saint Nicholas, Varuna
Message from Spirit: Stability, hope, and perseverance
Interpretation: The Anchor card indicates that Julien is currently facing challenges related to stability and security. Saint Nicholas, known for his generosity and support, encourages Julien to maintain hope and resilience despite any difficulties he may encounter. Varuna, the god of the sea, emphasizes the importance of endurance and faith in navigating turbulent

waters. Julien is urged to focus on establishing a solid foundation for himself, ensuring that he remains grounded while pursuing his aspirations.

Card 3: The Guidance or Strategy Provided by the Spirits: Tower (card 19)

Saint/deity: Saint Barbara, Brahma
Message from Spirit: Protection, boundaries, and order
Interpretation: The Tower card represents the need for protection and setting clear boundaries in Julien's life. Saint Barbara serves as a protective figure, reminding him to safeguard his interests and seek shelter from any potential threats. Brahma, as the god of creation, encourages Julien to establish order and structure in both his personal and professional realms. The spirits are guiding him to build a strong framework for his aspirations while ensuring he remains secure in his environment.

Julien's reading indicates a journey toward stability and clarity in his life. To achieve this, he should focus on fostering family bonds and pursuing knowledge. It's essential for him to cultivate resilience and hope, remaining steadfast in the face of challenges. The final card serves as a punctuation mark in his reading, providing a divine prescription: He should turn to Saint Barbara and Brahma for protection and structure. By doing so, Julien can create a safe environment in which he can truly thrive. Incorporating meditation into his routine can be a powerful means to achieve this sense of security and inner peace, allowing him to connect more deeply with the guidance of the spirits and navigate his path with confidence.

CHAPTER 9

Lenormand and Magical Rituals: Using the Cards as Tools for Manifestation

The use of playing cards in spell casting and magical work is an ancient practice that dates back centuries, long before specialized divination decks such as the Lenormand were created. The idea of using cards as a magical tool emerged naturally from their ability to represent different aspects of life, fate, and fortune. For many generations, both in formal occult settings and in folk traditions, playing cards have been used not only for divination but also as conduits of magical energy.

The suits, numbers, and court cards were often seen as symbols that could be activated to influence the spiritual and physical realms. For instance, the hearts suit was associated with emotions and relationships, clubs with physical energy and action, diamonds with wealth and material gain, and spades with challenges and protection. Practitioners would select specific cards to represent people, situations, or outcomes in their spell work, using them as focal points for ritualistic energy.

With the advent of the Lenormand deck in the nineteenth century, the tradition of using cards in magic took on a more structured and nuanced form. The Lenormand cards, with their detailed imagery and defined symbolism, provided a deeper layer of meaning, allowing for more-targeted and more-specific magical workings. Each Lenormand card carries a rich symbolic language that resonates with various aspects of life, from love and relationships to finances and personal power.

In magical rituals, Lenormand cards can act as powerful talismans or focus points for specific energies. The imagery on the cards aligns with the energies that practitioners wish to invoke, allowing them to connect more directly with their intentions. Unlike the abstract symbols on traditional playing cards, Lenormand cards depict tangible objects, people, and animals, making them easier to align with real-world situations in spell work.

For example, a card such as the Heart (24) represents love and can be used in rituals to attract romance or mend broken relationships. The Fish (34) can be used in prosperity spells, drawing abundance and financial success into one's life. The Tower (19) symbolizes protection and boundaries, making it ideal for rituals aimed at safeguarding oneself from harm or creating a secure environment.

Today, using Lenormand cards in magical rituals is a natural evolution of this ancient practice. When using Lenormand cards in spell work, the process usually begins by selecting cards that correspond to the desired outcome--often those cards would come up in a reading prior to the working. Just as with traditional playing cards, the chosen Lenormand cards act as the focal point of the ritual, representing the people, forces, or energies involved. The cards are often placed on an altar, surrounded by ritual objects such as candles, crystals, herbs, and personal items, to create a powerful symbolic arrangement that aligns with the practitioner's intention.

For instance, in a reconciliation spell, the Man (28), Woman (29), and Heart (24) cards would be used to represent the individuals involved and the love that is being rekindled. These cards can be empowered through the use of candles, oils, and offerings, drawing upon the spiritual energies they symbolize to influence the desired outcome. The cards act both as symbolic representations of the situation and as magical tools that channel spiritual energy into the working.

It's important to keep a separate Lenormand deck specifically for spiritual workings, spells, and rituals. This ensures that the energies of the deck remain attuned to magical purposes without becoming muddled by everyday readings. Over time, this deck will absorb the energy and intention of your rituals, becoming more powerful and aligned with your spiritual goals. The deck at the back of this book can be used in your spell work.

Additionally, in certain spells, the card itself may need to be buried with other spell ingredients, such as herbs, candles, or written petitions. In these cases, if you don't wish to sacrifice a card from your deck, you can draw or design a representation of the card to use in the spell. This allows you to preserve your main spiritual deck while still honoring the ritual's requirements. By creating these special tools, you reinforce your connection to the energies you're working with, enhancing the power and focus of your magical workings.

Spiritual Working 1: "Come to Me" (Reconciliation Spell)

One example of using Lenormand cards in magic is a reconciliation spell, also known as a "Come to Me" spell. The goal of this spell is to bring two people back together, whether it be for healing a romantic relationship, resolving a misunderstanding, or simply rekindling a connection. In this spell, the following Lenormand cards are used:

- The Man (28): Representing the masculine energy or the person in the relationship who identifies with the male figure
- The Woman (29): Representing the feminine energy or the person in the relationship who identifies with the female figure
- The Heart (24): Symbolizing love, passion, and emotional connection

These three cards work as the central focus of the ritual, representing the individuals involved and the love or affection that exists between them.

Materials Needed for the Ritual

To perform the reconciliation spell, gather the following materials:

- A red candle: Red symbolizes passion, love, and reconciliation. This candle should be dressed with oils that promote love and attraction, such as rose, jasmine, or patchouli.
- Rose petals: Rose petals are a classic symbol of love and romance. They help amplify the loving energy of the spell.
- Honey or sugar: To "sweeten" the situation, encouraging the people involved to be more kind, forgiving, and open to reconciliation.

Personal items: These can be photos, locks of hair, or items that belong to the individuals for whom the spell is being cast.

Incense: Love-related incense such as rose or sandalwood to create a sacred atmosphere.

Steps for the Ritual

1. Create a sacred space: Cleanse your space by burning sage or incense, ensuring that negative or stagnant energy is cleared.
2. Place the Lenormand cards: Arrange the Man, the Woman, and the Heart cards in a triangle on your altar or workspace, symbolizing the individuals and the relationship.
3. Dress the red candle: Anoint it with a love oil, visualizing the two individuals coming together in harmony.
4. Personalize the spell: Add personal items near the cards to make the connection stronger.
5. Scatter rose petals and honey: Drip honey and scatter rose petals, symbolizing sweetness and reconciliation.
6. Light the candle: As you light the candle, state your intention clearly.
7. Visualize the outcome: Spend time seeing the relationship healed and rekindled.
8. Let the candle burn: Allow it to burn down fully, releasing your intention into the universe.
9. Bury the remnants: Symbolize planting the seeds of reconciliation by burying any remaining materials in a garden.

Spiritual Working 2: Lucky Talisman Spell with the Clover Card

The Clover (2) card in Lenormand symbolizes luck, opportunities, and fortunate surprises. Its energy is light and fleeting but potent for attracting small bursts of good fortune. Using the Clover card as a focus for spell work can help create a talisman designed to draw luck and prosperity to the bearer. Below is a spell to create a lucky talisman with this card.

Materials Needed for the Lucky Talisman

- The Clover card: Represents luck and opportunity

- A small green pouch: Green symbolizes luck, abundance, and positive energy.
- Cinnamon stick: This is known for attracting luck, success, and wealth.
- Pyrite crystal: Often used in spells for prosperity and protection, pyrite is a powerful magnet for abundance.
- A small gold coin or charm: Gold symbolizes wealth and good fortune.
- Lucky oil: Use oils associated with luck, such as patchouli, basil, or bay leaf oil, to anoint the talisman and strengthen its energy.

Steps for Creating the Lucky Talisman

1. Cleanse the Clover card and items: To ensure that the talisman is filled with positive energy, begin by cleansing the Clover card and the other materials, using incense or smudging with sage or sandalwood. This clears away any stagnant energy.
2. Set your intention: Hold the Clover card in your hands and focus on the intention of attracting luck. Visualize yourself experiencing good fortune in all areas of life—whether it's in career, finances, or personal matters. Say a simple affirmation, such as "Luck flows into my life easily and brings me success and opportunity."
3. Anoint the Clover card: Take your chosen lucky oil and gently anoint the Clover card. As you do this, visualize the card becoming a beacon for luck, attracting positive energy into your life.
4. Place the items in the pouch: Place the Clover card, the cinnamon stick, the pyrite crystal, and the small gold coin or charm inside the green pouch. As you place each item in the pouch, state aloud your intention: "This talisman brings luck and fortune to me."
5. Charge the talisman with energy: Once all the items are in the pouch, hold it in both hands. Close your eyes and imagine the pouch glowing with a golden, radiant light. See this light drawing in luck, prosperity, and positive opportunities from the universe. You can chant or recite an affirmation like "This talisman brings me luck and opportunity. Fortune comes my way effortlessly."
6. Carry the talisman with you: Keep the pouch with you—whether in your pocket, purse, or worn around your neck as a constant source of luck. Use it especially when you need an extra boost of good fortune, such as before important meetings, interviews, or significant life events.

Recharging the Talisman

To keep the talisman's energy strong, you can periodically anoint it with a drop of your lucky oil or hold it in your hands while repeating your affirmations. You can also place it under the light of the full moon to recharge its power, keeping the energy fresh and potent.

Spiritual Working 3: Job Interview or Examination Success Spell

When preparing for a job interview, examination, or any situation requiring focus and clarity, this spell can help you attract favorable outcomes and boost confidence. The following spell will help you align with success, confidence, and sharp intellect. Keep in mind that as magical as this spell is, one should study and prepare to ensure success—the spell will work only if it matches your physical efforts.

Materials Needed for the Spell

- Key (33) card: Represents solutions, opportunities, and success
- Book (26) card: Symbolizes knowledge, wisdom, and preparation
- Sun (31) card: Represents success, confidence, and energy
- A yellow candle: Symbolizes intellect, focus, and success
- Bay leaves: Known for wisdom and success in academic or career-related matters
- Pen and paper: To write down your goal, such as the job title or exam you're preparing for
- Success oil: An oil blend for success (such as frankincense, bergamot, or cinnamon oil)

Steps for the Job Interview or Exam Success Spell

1. Cleanse your materials: Start by cleansing the Key, Book, and Sun cards along with the other items, using incense or sage or by passing them through the flame of the yellow candle. This clears any negative energy and opens the space for success and positive outcomes.
2. Set your intention: Take the Key card and hold it in your hands, visualizing the upcoming interview or exam. Focus on the result you want—visualize yourself acing the interview or exam with confidence and grace. Say out loud: "I unlock success and opportunity. The path to my goal is open and clear."
3. Anoint the cards and candle: Using your success oil, anoint the Key, Book, and Sun cards. Next, anoint the yellow candle, which symbolizes clarity, focus, and success. As you do this, imagine each item becoming charged with the energy to help you succeed.
4. Write down your goal: On a piece of paper, write down your specific goal—for instance, the name of the job or the exam you're preparing for. Fold the paper and place it under the yellow candle.
5. Create a focus area with the cards: Arrange the Key, Book, and Sun cards around the candle. The Key card represents unlocking the opportunity (the interview or exam), the Book card embodies the knowledge and preparation needed, and the Sun card brings success, confidence, and a favorable outcome.
6. Light the candle: As you light the yellow candle, say the following affirmation:"I am prepared, I am confident, and I am worthy of success. The doors of opportunity open before me. Knowledge and clarity guide my way, and I shine brightly in this moment. With the help of these energies, I attract a successful outcome."
7. Burn the bay leaves: Take one or more bay leaves and write the word "success" on them. As you burn the leaves in the candle flame, visualize the success coming to you—whether it's nailing the interview or passing the exam with flying colors. Feel your confidence growing as the leaves burn away.
8. Meditate on the cards: Spend a few moments focusing on each of the Lenormand cards. Let the Key card remind you that the path is open, the Book card remind you that you have the knowledge

and preparation, and the Sun card remind you of the success and confidence you will carry into the moment.

9. Close the ritual: Once you feel ready, let the candle burn for a little while longer, or extinguish it if you prefer. Keep the paper with your goal in a safe place, or carry it with you to the interview or exam for added confidence.

After the Spell

- For the interview: On the day of the interview, you can carry a printout or a small representation of the Key card with you as a charm. The Key symbolizes that you are unlocking your potential and opportunity.
- For the exam: If taking an exam, consider keeping the Book card with you for mental focus and preparation.

Recharging for Future Use

You can use the same cards for future interviews or exams. To recharge their energy, repeat the ritual or anoint them with oil when needed. You can also meditate on these cards before significant events to strengthen your connection to the energies they represent.

CHAPTER 10

Lenormand in Portugal: A Mysterious Arrival

When the Lenormand oracle first arrived in Portugal, its origins were shrouded in mystery, as often happens with mystical objects and practices. The cards quickly became popular, but their true beginnings were largely unknown to those who used them. In fact, across many countries where the Lenormand deck spread, its origins were either misunderstood or deliberately obscured. Myths and legends surrounded the cards, adding to their mystical allure.

In Portugal, it was widely believed that the Lenormand oracle had been brought by the Gypsies, a nomadic people known for their psychic abilities and their deep connection to the mystical arts. Because of this, the Lenormand deck became known locally as the Baralho Cigano, which translates to "Gypsy deck" in English. This name reflected the belief that the deck was of Gypsy origin, carried by the Romani people during their migration through Europe, including into Portugal.

The Romani, often referred to as Gypsies, have long been associated with magic, fortune-telling, and a wandering lifestyle. Originating from northern India, the Romani people spread across Europe and beyond, adapting to local cultures while maintaining their own customs and traditions. Along the way, they became known for their deep psychic abilities, their skill in reading the future, and their powerful use of cartomancy, palmistry, and other divination techniques. In Portugal, the Romani were viewed with both fascination and suspicion. They were seen as powerful witches, capable of seeing beyond the veil of the mundane world into the spiritual and magical realms. For many, their reputation as psychics and fortune-tellers was solidified by their use of cards, especially those resembling the Lenormand deck. Whether they actually introduced the Lenormand cards to Portugal or simply popularized them through their reputation as mystics remains unclear, but the association stuck.

Even today, the legend of the Lenormand oracle's Gypsy origins persists in certain parts of Portugal. Many readers still view the deck as something that transcends culture and time, its images speaking a language that is both ancient and timeless. Some even feel that the cards carry the wisdom of the Romani people, who, despite their persecution throughout history, have managed to preserve their spiritual knowledge.

The Lenormand deck, whether seen as Gypsy in origin or not, has become a key tool in the practice of Portuguese cartomancy. Readers who use the deck today often blend its traditional meanings with local customs and spiritual beliefs, just as the Gypsies might have done centuries before.

The result is a unique blend of fortune-telling traditions, one where the Lenormand cards carry both a local and universal significance. Whether or not the deck truly arrived with the Gypsies, their mystique and spiritual influence have undeniably shaped how the Lenormand is viewed and used in Portugal.

CHAPTER 11

Lenormand's Journey Across the Atlantic

As we explored in the previous chapter, the Lenormand deck journeyed from France to various parts of the world, carried by waves of migration, colonization, and cultural exchange. One such journey brought Lenormand to the shores of Brazil, carried by Portuguese settlers and travelers. Just as the deck made its way to places such as Réunion Island during French colonization, it also found new life in Brazil, where it blended with the rich tapestry of Brazilian spiritual and cultural practices.

Brazil, once a colony of Portugal, shared deep cultural, religious, and social ties with its European counterpart. These connections meant that much of what became popular in Portugal, including spiritual practices, eventually found its way to Brazil. The Lenormand oracle, known in Portugal as the Baralho Cigano (Gypsy deck), was no exception.

During the nineteenth century, as Portuguese settlers and immigrants made their way to Brazil, they brought with them not only their language, religion, and traditions but also their mystical tools, such as the Lenormand deck. The cards, already woven into Portuguese fortune-telling and spiritual practices, took on new life in the Brazilian landscape, where they would eventually become a crucial part of local cartomancy. Brazil has always been a land of cultural and spiritual diversity. As Portuguese colonizers brought Catholicism and European traditions, the enslaved Africans brought their own powerful spiritual systems, including Candomblé and

Umbanda, while the Indigenous peoples of Brazil held their own sacred beliefs and practices. Over time, these various traditions mixed, creating a unique spiritual landscape where Catholic saints, African orishas, and Indigenous spirits often coexisted in harmony.

When the Baralho Cigano arrived in Brazil, it found itself absorbed into this melting pot of beliefs. Just as it had been adapted in Portugal to reflect the Romani people's mystical influence, in Brazil the Lenormand deck was once again syncretized with local spiritual practices. The cards began to carry multiple layers of meaning, intertwining Catholic symbolism with African and Indigenous spiritual elements. In the Brazilian context, the deck was not only a tool for fortune-telling but also a bridge between the various spiritual forces at play.

The Brazilian School of Lenormand

As we've seen with the concept of "schools" in Lenormand, the deck's meanings and uses can vary between different traditions. Much like the German and French schools of cartomancy, the Brazilian school of Lenormand has developed its unique interpretations and practices. The European tradition of Lenormand, particularly the French and German schools, focuses heavily on the cards' literal meanings and their combinations to form predictive readings.

Certain cards, in particular, illustrate this divergence in meaning, reflecting the Brazilian cultural landscape and spiritual beliefs.

Here are a few notable examples:

- The Clover (2): In the European tradition, the Clover is often associated with luck, chance, and unexpected opportunities. However, in the Brazilian context, the Clover may be interpreted as an obstacle or a sign of misfortune. It can represent a lack of opportunity or an indication that luck is not on the querent's side at the moment. This reversal highlights the belief that what may seem fortunate can often be deceptive, emphasizing the need for caution and mindfulness in decisions.
- The Snake (7): While the Snake card is generally linked to deceit and betrayal in European readings, in Brazil it takes on additional layers of meaning. The Cobra, as it is often referred to, embodies themes

of sexuality and temptation. This association draws parallels to the biblical story of Eve being tempted by the snake to eat the forbidden fruit, connecting the Cobra to ideas of seduction, desire, and the complexities of human relationships. It serves as a reminder to be wary of temptations that may lead to moral or emotional peril.

- The Cross (36): In the European school, the Cross is typically associated with burdens, suffering, and the trials of life. However, within the Brazilian tradition, the Cross symbolizes victory after hardship. It reflects a sense of resurrection and renewal, suggesting that the querent has the opportunity to rise above their challenges and emerge stronger. This interpretation emphasizes hope and resilience, indicating that through suffering, there can be growth, transformation, and a chance to do better.

A Warning Before Proceeding

Before delving further into this chapter, I feel it is crucial to share something deeply important. As I've mentioned in previous chapters, especially when discussing my island, Réunion, and its rich spirituality, all the spiritual workings I've shared were done with permission from my guides. I approached each subject with reverence and care, ensuring that I had the necessary blessings to pass this knowledge along to you. Now, I ask the same of you: to treat this knowledge with the utmost respect and ethical consideration.

As we delve into the Brazilian tradition, especially where it intersects with Orishas, Exus, and other spiritual entities, I implore you once more to approach with reverence. What I am sharing here is not just historical information but the culmination of years of personal investigation into Lenormand, and countless conversations with Brazilian practitioners, spiritual leaders, and ordinary people.

The purpose of this chapter is not to prescribe or reduce these practices to simple card meanings. Rather, it is to provide insight into the rich and evolving spiritual landscape surrounding Lenormand. In divination, no system remains fixed—it changes with time, tradition, and location. The Brazilian tradition of Lenormand is a living testament to this transformation.

If you seek to work with the spiritual aspects of the Lenormand deck, particularly where it relates to Orishas and Exus, I advise you to proceed only if you are properly initiated. This is not merely a set of card meanings but a philosophy, a profound legacy embedded within the cards. To approach these spiritual forces without the proper training and reverence would be not only disrespectful but potentially dangerous. Therefore, let us continue with open minds, deep respect, and a genuine desire to honor the cultures and traditions that have shaped this system.

In contrast, the Brazilian tradition often incorporates mysticism, spirituality, and symbolism that is specific to Afro-Brazilian and Catholic syncretism, blending elements of Umbanda and Candomblé into their readings.

While the European schools might assign relatively neutral meanings to some cards, the Brazilian approach often layers these meanings with deeper spiritual significance. For example:

The Cross (36): In the European tradition, the Cross typically represents burdens, suffering, or heavy responsibility. However, in the Brazilian school, the Cross is not only a card of hardship but also a card of faith. It symbolizes one's spiritual journey and the sacrifices required for growth, reflecting influences both from Catholicism and Afro-Brazilian beliefs. The Cross encourages resilience and trust in divine guidance during challenges.

The Ship (3): Traditionally a card of travel and movement, in the Brazilian context the Ship is closely associated with Yemanjá, the orisha of the sea and motherhood. This connection imbues the card with emotional depth, intuition, and the ability to navigate life's emotional tides. In readings, the Ship may signify a journey of self-discovery, healing, or spiritual growth, guided by Yemanjá's nurturing energy.

The Tree (5): The Tree, representing health, growth, and well-being, is deeply linked to Oxóssi, the orisha of the forest, hunting, and abundance. In the Brazilian tradition, the Tree reflects not only physical health but also spiritual vitality and a harmonious relationship with nature. Oxóssi's energy encourages the seeker to cultivate wisdom, embrace abundance, and stay grounded while pursuing their goals. The Tree in this context also serves as a reminder of the interconnectedness of life and the healing power of nature.

In the Petit Lenormand, not all cards are associated with an Orisha; only about half the deck carries a spiritual connection to these benevolent beings. The following insights were graciously shared by practitioners of Candomblé and Umbanda, whom I am honored to call friends.

It is important to approach this resource with respect and reverence. For those who wish to delve deeper into this spirituality, proper initiation is essential to ensure an authentic and meaningful connection.

THE RIDER: EXU

Exu is one of the most significant and dynamic Orishas in the Yoruba religion and its Afro-Brazilian counterparts, such as Candomblé, Umbanda, and Quimbanda. He is considered the messenger of the gods, the guardian of pathways, and the protector of communication, both in the material and spiritual worlds. Exu plays a pivotal role in the spiritual and daily lives of practitioners, serving as an intermediary between humans and the divine.

Key attributes and symbolism:

- Messenger of the Orishas: Exu is the primary intermediary between the human world and the Orishas. He facilitates communication between humans and the divine, carrying messages and prayers to the gods and bringing their guidance back to people.
- Guardian of the crossroads: Exu is known as the Orisha of the crossroads, which symbolizes his ability to open paths, create opportunities, and navigate between different realms. He is often invoked when one is at a crossroads in life, seeking direction or transformation.
- Duality and balance: Exu is often seen as a dual figure, embodying both positive and negative qualities. This duality reflects his ability both to challenge and protect, creating the balance between order and chaos, good and bad, which is necessary for spiritual evolution.

Roles and functions:

1. Protector and guide: Exu acts as a protector of practitioners and communities, safeguarding them from negative energies, malicious spirits, and harmful forces. He is also invoked to clear obstacles, remove blockages, and create new openings for progress.
2. Mediator in rituals: In religious ceremonies, Exu is often the first spirit to be called upon, since h0e is the one who opens the spiritual pathways for communication with the other Orishas. Without Exu's intervention, no ritual can proceed successfully.

3. God of communication and justice: Exu's role as a communicator means he can be invoked to help with negotiations, conflicts, and communication in human affairs. He is also linked to justice, ensuring that karmic balance is maintained in both the spiritual and material worlds.

THE SHIP AND THE ANCHOR: YEMANJÁ

Yemanjá is the Orisha of the sea, motherhood, and fertility, and the protector of all living beings. Yemanjá holds an essential place both in the spiritual and cultural life of practitioners, representing love, protection, and the nurturing power of water.

Key attributes and symbolism:

- Mother of All: Yemanjá is known as the mother of all Orishas and the mother of humanity. She is often referred to as "Mãe de Todos" (Mother of All), symbolizing her deep nurturing qualities and her connection to all life forms. Her maternal energy extends to both the human realm and the spiritual world.
- Orisha of the sea: Yemanjá rules over the oceans, and all bodies of water. Water is seen as the source of life, and Yemanjá embodies its life-giving and cleansing powers. She is believed to control the tides, the flow of water, and all the creatures that live in the sea.
- Fertility and motherhood: As the goddess of fertility, Yemanjá is closely associated with the birth of children, pregnancy, and nurturing. She represents maternal love, care, and protection, ensuring the well-being of mothers and children. Yemanjá's energy supports the creation and growth of life, both physical and spiritual.
- Healing and emotional cleansing: Yemanjá is also regarded as a healer, using the power of water to cleanse and purify emotional wounds. Her energy is invoked in times of emotional distress or when a person needs healing and restoration. The ocean is seen as a place of emotional release, and Yemanjá's power helps cleanse negative energies, bringing peace and tranquility.

Roles and functions:

1. Protector of women and children: Yemanjá is particularly revered by women, especially those in childbirth or motherhood. She is called upon to protect and guide mothers, ensuring the safety of their children and their well-being. Women often seek her blessings for fertility and maternal protection.
2. Orisha of love and compassion: Yemanjá embodies unconditional love and compassion. She is invoked during rituals for emotional healing, to bring harmony and balance in relationships, and for the protection of the family. Yemanjá's love is seen as all-encompassing, gentle, and nurturing.
3. Goddess of transformation: As an Orisha of water, Yemanjá is closely associated with emotional and spiritual transformation. Water is symbolic of change and fluidity, and Yemanjá guides individuals through personal transformations, helping them let go of negative emotions, past trauma, and obstacles.
4. Guardian of the seas and marine life: Yemanjá is also a protector of the marine world and its creatures. As the goddess of the sea, she governs the harmony of the ecosystem, ensuring the well-being of the creatures and the environment.

THE TREE: OXÓSSI

Oxóssi is the Orisha of the forest, hunting, and abundance, and the guardian of the natural world. Oxóssi is celebrated for his wisdom, intelligence, and mastery of survival in the wilderness. He is considered the protector of the hunters, as well as a symbol of resourcefulness, prosperity, and connection to nature.

Key attributes and symbolism:

- The Hunter: Oxóssi is often depicted as a skilled hunter, armed with a bow and arrow. His connection to hunting symbolizes the quest for sustenance, survival, and the skillful use of natural resources. As the master hunter, he is also linked to the preservation and balance of the natural environment.

- Abundance and prosperity: Oxóssi is associated with abundance, particularly in relation to food, resources, and wealth. He is seen as the Orisha who brings prosperity and ensures that his followers are provided for. In this role, he embodies the idea that careful planning, wisdom, and connection with nature lead to material success.
- Wisdom and intelligence: Oxóssi is also known for his intellectual strength. He is a wise figure who provides guidance and insight to those who seek him out. His intelligence helps his devotees navigate life's challenges, ensuring they have the resources and knowledge to succeed.
- Guardian of the forest: As the Orisha of the forest, Oxóssi is deeply connected to nature, especially the woods, rivers, and wildlife. He is a protector of the environment and is invoked for matters related to nature conservation and the respect of the land and its creatures.

Roles and functions:

1. Protector of hunters and gatherers: Oxóssi is the patron Orisha of hunters, foragers, and anyone who works with nature to provide for themselves and others. He teaches the values of respect for the land and its resources, and his energy supports those who seek sustenance from the natural world.
2. Bringer of abundance and good fortune: As an Orisha of prosperity, Oxóssi is called upon to ensure that individuals and families have enough food, wealth, and resources. He is considered a powerful force in ensuring material success, and his blessings are sought for financial stability and abundance.
3. Symbol of strength and survival: Oxóssi represents resilience and the ability to overcome adversity. He embodies the survival instinct that is essential to human and animal life, and he provides guidance to help people navigate difficult times and persevere in challenging circumstances.

THE CLOUDS: IANSÃ

Iansã is the Orisha of winds, storms, and transformation, and the guardian of the cemetery. Iansã is known for her fierce energy, her role in bringing change, and her ability to protect and guide her followers with courage and strength.

Key attributes and symbolism:

- The winds and storms: Iansã is often depicted as the goddess of the winds and storms. She controls the forces of nature, particularly the strong winds and violent storms that signify power and transformation. She is associated with movement, change, and the uncontrollable aspects of life.
- Transformation and change: As a transformative Orisha, Iansã represents both destruction and renewal. She has the power to bring about significant changes, clearing the path for new beginnings. Her energy is invoked for personal transformation, breaking free from the past, and embracing new opportunities.
- Strength and courage: Iansã is known for her courageous and bold nature. She embodies the strength to face life's challenges head on and encourages her followers to act with determination, especially in times of adversity. Her warrior spirit is inspiring, urging her devotees to stand firm in their beliefs and convictions.

Roles and functions:

1. Bringer of transformation and new beginnings: Iansã is invoked when individuals or communities seek significant changes in their lives. She helps clear obstacles and brings the necessary energy to transform situations, whether personal, spiritual, or material. Her power is about embracing change and trusting the process.
2. Goddess of the storms and nature's forces: As the master of winds and storms, Iansã brings the energy needed to break barriers and initiate change. She is also a protective force against negative spiritual energies. Her storms may symbolize cleansing and the destruction of the old to make way for the new.

3. Warrior spirit and defender: Iansã is revered for her warrior qualities. She symbolizes courage and strength, particularly in the face of adversity. She empowers her followers to stand up for themselves and others, to fight for justice, and to act with boldness and conviction in their pursuits.

THE COFFIN: OMULU

Omulu is the Orisha of disease, healing, life cycles, and the earth. Omulu is both feared and revered, since he governs the forces of illness, but he is also a powerful healer and protector, particularly in matters related to health, purification, and death.

Key attributes and symbolism:

- Master of disease and healing: Omulu is deeply connected to illness, especially contagious diseases, as well as the process of healing and purification. He has the power to bring both sickness and cure, and he is often invoked to heal ailments and to provide protection from illness.
- The earth and fertility: Omulu is associated with the earth and its cycles, representing the power of the soil and nature. He is often seen as a life giver, providing sustenance and fertility. His energy is linked to the cycles of life and death, as well as the rebirth and regeneration that comes from the earth.
- The death and rebirth cycles: Omulu governs the cycle of life, death, and reincarnation. While he is closely linked to death and the end of life, he also brings the possibility of regeneration, healing, and renewal. His role is essential for the balance of life and death, as well as the spiritual cleansing of individuals.

Roles and functions:

1. Protector against disease and illness: Omulu is called upon for protection from illness, especially contagious diseases. His energy is invoked to heal both physical and spiritual ailments, and his presence is sought for purification, cleansing, and protection against negative forces that may cause harm to one's health.

2. Healer and regenerator: As a healer, Omulu plays an important role in bringing healing and recovery to those suffering from physical or emotional distress. He is often invoked during healing rituals and ceremonies aimed at restoring health and vitality. His power is also tied to the regeneration of life, making him a key Orisha in rituals focused on spiritual renewal.
3. Guardian of the earth and ancestors: Omulu's association with the earth makes him a guardian of both the natural world and the ancestral spirits. He is invoked to protect the land, ensure fertility, and provide for the well-being of the community. He also watches over the spirits of the ancestors, assisting in their safe passage to the afterlife and their continued guidance for the living.
4. Orisha of death and transition: Omulu governs the process of death and the transition from the physical to the spiritual realm. He is invoked to guide the souls of the departed and ensure their peaceful transition. His presence is called upon in funerary rituals and ceremonies to honor and guide the spirits of the deceased.

THE BOUQUET: NANÃ BULUKU

Nanã Buluku is the elder Orisha of wisdom and the earth. Revered as one of the most ancient and powerful figures in the Yoruba tradition and Afro-Brazilian practices such as Candomblé and Umbanda, Nanã embodies ancestral knowledge, patience, and forgiveness. She is deeply associated with creation, fertility, the primordial waters, and the cycles of life, death, and rebirth.

Key attributes and symbolism:

- Ancestral knowledge: Nanã represents the wisdom of the ancestors and the keeper of the secrets of the earth. As a symbol of ancient knowledge, she is seen as a source of guidance and spiritual insight, offering clarity on the mysteries of life and death.
- Patience and forgiveness: Nanã is known for her calm, nurturing energy. She embodies patience and the ability to forgive, helping to heal emotional wounds and restore balance in relationships.

- Earth and fertility: Nanã governs the earth, particularly the fertile soils, marshes, and swamps, which symbolize her power over fertility and creation. She nurtures life, ensuring the growth of crops, healthful childbirth, and the natural cycles of the world.
- Primordial waters: As the Orisha of the primordial waters, Nanã is deeply connected to the life-giving force of water. Her waters represent the origin of all life, carrying transformative power that brings both life and death, symbolizing the balance of creation and destruction.

Roles and functions:

1. Protector of fertility and life: Nanã is invoked for matters of fertility, both in terms of human reproduction and agricultural success. She is called upon to ensure the birth of healthy children and the prosperity of crops, as well as to maintain the balance of nature.
2. Source of wisdom and spiritual guidance: Nanã is a revered figure of wisdom, offering spiritual clarity and guidance. She assists those seeking to understand deeper truths and navigate life's challenges with patience and insight.
3. Guardian of ancestral wisdom: Nanã is also the guardian of the ancestral spirits, ensuring their wisdom is passed down and honored through generations. She is invoked in rituals of ancestor veneration and spiritual connection, helping to maintain the lineage of wisdom and knowledge.

THE SICKLE OR SCYTHE: Ọ̀BÀLÚA

Ọbàlúa (also known as Obaluayê) is recognized primarily as the Orisha of health, disease, and healing and is deeply connected to the cycles of life and death, making him a powerful and complex figure in African diasporic spiritual traditions.

Key attributes and symbolism:

- Master of disease and healing: Ọbàlúa is closely associated with both illness and healing. He is believed to have the power to cause illness, particularly infectious diseases, but also the power to heal and restore balance. His role as both a bringer of illness and a healer reflects the dual nature of life and death, sickness and health.

- The earth and purification: Ọbàlúa is a protector of the earth and is linked to its fertile aspects. He is often associated with the earth's power to purify, transform, and regenerate. His energy is seen as essential for cleansing both physical and spiritual impurities, making him an important figure in purification rituals.
- Life, death, and rebirth: Ọbàlúa governs the cycle of life, death, and rebirth. He is the force that oversees the transition between life and the afterlife, ensuring that the process is respected, and that the soul's journey is guided. His energy symbolizes the constant cycles of life and the inevitability of death, as well as the opportunities for renewal and regeneration.

Roles and functions:

1. Protector and healer: Ọbàlúa is revered for his role in healing. He is invoked for matters related to physical illness, especially those caused by contagious diseases. He is also called upon for spiritual cleansing and protection, since his energy can purify negative forces and restore harmony and health.
2. Guardian of the earth: As an Orisha associated with the earth, Ọbàlúa governs the processes of growth, decay, and transformation. He is invoked for rituals related to agriculture, the fertility of the land, and the balance of nature. His connection to the earth also makes him a powerful figure in rituals aimed at enhancing the community's prosperity and well-being.
3. Spiritual transformation: Ọbàlúa is deeply tied to the processes of spiritual transformation, particularly those that involve purification. He is called upon during rites of passage, such as birth, initiation, and death, to guide individuals through the transformative stages of life. His energy is essential for the cleansing and renewal of both body and spirit.

THE STARS: ORUNMILA

Orunmila is the Orisha of wisdom, knowledge, and divination and is considered the deity of understanding and foresight. Orunmila is the guardian of the knowledge of the universe and is often invoked for guidance and clarity in times of uncertainty.

Key attributes and symbolism:

- Wisdom and knowledge: Orunmila is the embodiment of divine wisdom and knowledge. He is seen as the Orisha who understands the past, present, and future. His knowledge of the universe encompasses all aspects of life, from human affairs to cosmic order. He is also associated with the concept of "Ifá," the Yoruba system of divination, which is based on interpreting the wisdom of the universe through symbols, rituals, and sacred texts.
- Divination and prophecy: As the Orisha of divination, Orunmila is the principal deity consulted for guidance in Yoruba spirituality. Through the Ifá divination system, practitioners seek his wisdom to understand the paths of their lives, make decisions, and align with their destiny. Orunmila's messages come through oracles, priests, and ceremonies that interpret the divine will.
- The memory of the universe: Orunmila is also known as the "witness" of the cosmos, having witnessed the creation of the world and possessing the knowledge of all things. He is believed to hold the records of human experiences, past lives, and spiritual truths. This knowledge is transmitted through the Ifá tradition and passed down to his followers.

Roles and functions:

1. Diviner and guide: Orunmila is invoked by practitioners of Ifá to offer insight into the future and to provide answers to life's most-pressing questions. As the divine source of wisdom, he is consulted for advice on matters such as love, health, career, and spiritual direction. Through divination, his guidance is sought to ensure that individuals make choices aligned with their destiny.
2. Guardian of destiny: Orunmila is considered the custodian of human destiny and fate. He is believed to know each person's true path in life and can help reveal it through divination. This divine

knowledge allows individuals to make informed decisions and avoid obstacles that could hinder their progress.

3. Wisdom and teaching: Orunmila is revered as a teacher who imparts the deep spiritual knowledge of the universe. He is often associated with the transmission of sacred knowledge, and his followers seek him out to learn the mysteries of life, the secrets of the divine, and how to align with cosmic laws.
4. Protector of knowledge: Orunmila is also the protector of sacred wisdom and spiritual truths. In the Yoruba tradition, only initiated priests and diviners who undergo extensive training are able to access Orunmila's wisdom and perform Ifá divinations. This ensures that his teachings are preserved and shared with respect and reverence.
5. Spiritual counselor: As a spiritual counselor, Orunmila provides clarity and guidance to individuals seeking answers. Whether through direct divination or indirect teachings, he helps people navigate challenges, heal spiritual wounds, and find peace by aligning with their true purpose in life.

THE GARDEN: OSSAIN

Ossain is the deity of the forest, herbs, and healing and is considered the guardian of medicinal plants and natural remedies. Ossain is deeply connected to the earth, nature, and the power of plants to cure physical and spiritual ailments.

Key attributes and symbolism:

- The Orịsha of herbs and healing: Ossain is the master of medicinal plants and is revered for his deep knowledge of the healing properties of herbs. He is called upon for health-related matters and is believed to provide the wisdom necessary to heal ailments through natural remedies. In many traditions, he is also invoked in rituals for spiritual purification and protection.
- The forest and nature: Ossain is considered a protector of the forest and all the natural forces of the earth. He is associated with the abundance of nature, the cycles of growth, and the energy that sustains life. His realm includes not only the physical forests but also the spiritual essence of all plants and the wisdom that lies within them.

Roles and functions:

1. Guardian of healing: Ossain is invoked primarily for healing purposes. He governs all forms of plant-based medicine and is believed to have the power to cure diseases and ailments, both physical and spiritual. His knowledge is essential for spiritual practitioners and herbalists who rely on the healing properties of nature.
2. Protector of nature: As the protector of the forest and all plant life, Ossain is closely linked to the preservation of the environment. He is considered an advocate for ecological balance and is called upon to ensure the protection of natural resources and ecosystems.
3. Spiritual purification: Ossain is also invoked for purification rituals. His energy is believed to cleanse individuals from negative energies, spiritual blockages, and imbalances. By using plants in rituals and ceremonies, practitioners seek to harmonize their spiritual and physical health.

THE MOUNTAIN: XANGÔ

Xangô is one of the most powerful and revered Orishas. He is the deity of thunder, lightning, fire, justice, and masculinity. Xangô is associated with strength, power, and leadership and is considered a warrior king who governs over the forces of nature and divine law.

Key attributes and symbolism:

- Thunder and lightning: Xangô is the Orisha of thunder and lightning, and his presence is symbolized by these powerful natural forces. He controls the weather and is believed to use his lightning to strike down enemies or enemies of justice. His power over thunder represents his ability to bring both destruction and renewal.
- Justice and balance: Xangô is also the Orisha of justice, fairness, and balance. He is associated with the enforcement of divine law, ensuring that the principles of fairness and righteousness are upheld. In this role, he is seen as a protector of the weak and a defender of the oppressed.
- Fire and power: Xangô is often associated with fire, symbolizing transformation, strength, and vitality. Fire is a dual symbol for him,

representing both destruction and purification, since it can burn away impurities to make way for new growth.

Roles and functions:

1. Protector and warrior: Xangô is seen as a protector and a warrior who defends his followers from harm. He is called upon for strength in times of battle, whether physical or spiritual, and for protection against injustice and oppression. His role as a warrior king makes him a powerful figure in the spiritual and earthly realms.
2. Guardian of justice: Xangô is the embodiment of divine justice and fairness. He is invoked in cases of injustice, when individuals are wronged or when the truth must prevail. His energy is believed to bring clarity and fairness to difficult situations, helping to restore balance.
3. Symbol of masculinity and vitality: Xangô is the Orisha of masculinity, vitality, and virility. His energy is associated with male strength, endurance, and reproductive power. He is revered by men seeking to embody his qualities of strength, leadership, and determination.
4. Divine protector: Xangô's protective nature extends to his followers, shielding them from misfortune, bad luck, and spiritual harm. He is often called upon to provide divine protection and to remove obstacles in one's life, particularly those related to unjust situations.

THE PATHS: OGUM

Ogum is the Orisha of iron, tools, war, technology, and labor. Ogum is seen as a warrior and protector who governs over the forces of creation and innovation and the ability to overcome challenges through hard work and strength.

Key attributes and symbolism:

- Iron and tools: Ogum is associated primarily with iron, metalwork, and tools. He is the patron of blacksmiths, craftsmen, and engineers, since he governs over the creation and use of weapons, tools, and other objects made from iron and metal. His ability to shape and manipulate these materials symbolizes his power over creation and transformation.

- War and battle: As the Orisha of war and battle, Ogum represents courage, strength, and the power to fight against adversities. He is called upon by warriors, soldiers, and those who need protection or strength in times of conflict. His role as a warrior also connects him to the idea of justice, since he fights to protect the weak and uphold righteousness.
- Technology and innovation: Ogum is also associated with the development of technology and innovation. As a god of labor and progress, he governs over advancements in engineering, invention, and the use of machinery. He is revered as the divine force behind progress and technological breakthroughs, especially those that improve human life and work.

Roles and functions:

1. Warrior and protector: Ogum is a powerful warrior Orisha, often called upon for protection, strength, and victory in times of conflict. His energy is invoked in battles, whether physical or spiritual, to help overcome obstacles and enemies. He is seen as the defender of those in need and a champion of justice.
2. Patron of work and labor: Ogum is the Orisha of labor and perseverance. He is especially revered by workers, artisans, and those who rely on tools for their craft, such as blacksmiths, carpenters, builders, and engineers. He blesses them with the strength and skill needed to succeed in their labor, whether it's physical work or intellectual creation.
3. Divine inventor: As the Orisha of technology and progress, Ogum governs the development of tools, machines, and innovations that help humans overcome difficulties and advance in life. His influence is seen in fields of engineering, construction, and the creation of tools and technology.
4. Symbol of courage and strength: Ogum embodies the qualities of courage, determination, and endurance. He is invoked by those seeking to overcome challenges or obstacles, and his energy helps strengthen resolve and ensure perseverance in the face of adversity.
5. Guardian of justice: Ogum's role as a protector extends to upholding justice and fighting for fairness. His strength and leadership

make him a defender of the oppressed and a symbol of the power to fight against injustice.

6. Protector of roads and paths: In some traditions, Ogum is also believed to protect roads, paths, and journeys. He is seen as the Orisha who clears the way, removing obstacles and ensuring smooth passage for travelers and those embarking on new ventures or paths in life.

THE LILIES: OXUM

Oxum (also spelled Oshun) is one of the most beloved and revered Orishas in the Yoruba religion and its Afro-Brazilian traditions, including Candomblé and Umbanda. She is the Orisha of love, beauty, fertility, fresh waters, and prosperity. Oxum is associated with the nurturing aspects of femininity, compassion, and grace, as well as the material and spiritual abundance that flows from her influence.

Key attributes and symbolism:

- Fresh water and rivers: Oxum is the goddess of fresh waters, especially rivers, lakes, and streams. These waters symbolize life, healing, and purification. Oxum's domain is often associated with the nourishing and life-giving properties of water, which cleanses, sustains, and supports all living things.
- Love and beauty: As the Orisha of love, beauty, and sensuality, Oxum governs romantic relationships, the expression of love, and the allure of beauty in all its forms. She is invoked for matters of the heart, such as finding true love, maintaining harmonious relationships, or increasing one's sense of beauty and charm.
- Fertility and motherhood: Oxum is a protector of mothers, children, and fertility. She is called upon by women who seek to conceive, as well as by mothers who want to ensure the health and well-being of their children. Her nurturing and maternal qualities are central to her identity.
- Prosperity and abundance: Oxum is also associated with wealth, prosperity, and material abundance. Her blessings are often sought by those who wish to increase their financial well-being or attract

opportunities for success and growth. Oxum's energy flows through commerce, agriculture, and all areas where abundance and growth are desired.

Roles and functions:

1. Goddess of love and romance: Oxum is the divine force behind romantic relationships and the attraction of love. She governs the emotions of affection, passion, and romance, bringing harmony and warmth to the hearts of her devotees. She is often invoked to find love, heal broken relationships, or enhance feelings of closeness and intimacy.
2. Protector of women and children: Oxum is a maternal figure, offering protection and care to mothers, children, and pregnant women. She is called upon for blessings related to fertility, childbirth, and the well-being of children. Women often seek her assistance in matters related to motherhood and family life.
3. Goddess of fresh waters and healing: As the Orisha of fresh waters, Oxum's waters are said to have healing properties. She is invoked for physical and spiritual purification, as well as for protection against illness and negative energy. Her waters are seen as a source of renewal and rejuvenation.
4. Bringer of prosperity and abundance: Oxum is associated with the flow of prosperity and wealth. She is a patron of those involved in commerce, trade, and the pursuit of material wealth. Her blessings are often invoked to bring financial success, good fortune, and an abundance of resources into one's life.
5. Symbol of feminine energy and grace: Oxum embodies the qualities of feminine beauty, grace, and elegance. She is revered as a symbol of femininity in its highest and most divine form—gentle, loving, and powerful. Her followers seek to embody these qualities in their own lives, cultivating beauty, charm, and grace in their actions and relationships.
6. Divine mediator: Seen as a mediator and peacemaker, particularly in matters of the heart, Oxum is invoked to heal emotional wounds, resolve conflicts in relationships, and bring peace and harmony to those in turmoil.

THE SUN: OXALÁ

Oxalá is often considered the Orisha of creation, purity, peace, and justice, embodying the highest spiritual and divine energy in the pantheon. Oxalá is revered as the Orisha of light, harmony, and wisdom, representing the essence of divinity itself.

Key attributes and symbolism:

- Creation and the creator: Oxalá is associated with the creation of the world and all living beings. In some interpretations, he is regarded as the father of all Orishas, with his divine essence manifesting in the natural world and in every living thing. As the Orisha of creation, Oxalá is a symbol of the primordial forces that shape existence and give life.
- Purity and light: Oxalá is synonymous with purity, clarity, and the highest spiritual light. He embodies divine wisdom and holiness, often depicted in white clothing or as a figure of light. His presence is said to purify the mind, body, and spirit, helping his followers achieve balance and spiritual enlightenment.
- Peace and justice: As a peaceful and just Orisha, Oxalá is associated with harmony, fairness, and truth. He is invoked in times of conflict or injustice, bringing peace to situations of discord. Oxalá also represents the moral and ethical guidelines that govern the human soul, emphasizing compassion, integrity, and wisdom.
- Wisdom and guidance: Oxalá is considered the embodiment of divine wisdom and guidance. His followers seek his wisdom to navigate life's challenges and seek clarity in times of uncertainty. He is revered for his ability to bring understanding and light into the lives of his devotees, helping them connect with higher knowledge and spiritual insight.

Roles and functions:

1. Orisha of creation: Oxalá is credited with the creation of humanity and the world. As a divine architect, he shapes the universe and breathes life into all beings. He is the source of all creation, and his energy permeates everything, from the stars in the sky to the earth beneath our feet.

2. Embodiment of purity: Oxalá's purity is one of his defining qualities. He is invoked to purify the soul, cleanse negative energies, and bring clarity to the mind. Rituals dedicated to Oxalá focus on purification and spiritual renewal, helping devotees reconnect with their divine essence.
3. Bringer of peace and justice: Oxalá is a symbol of peace and justice in the Yoruba pantheon. He is called upon to resolve conflicts, restore balance, and promote fairness. His energy is invoked in legal matters, disputes, and any situation requiring a sense of moral clarity and resolution.
4. Divine wisdom and guidance: As the Orisha of wisdom, Oxalá offers spiritual guidance and insight to his followers. He is sought after for his ability to bring understanding, clarity, and enlightenment, particularly when faced with difficult decisions or challenging circumstances. Devotees believe that Oxalá helps them align with their higher purpose and divine plan.
5. Spiritual leader: Oxalá is often seen as the spiritual leader of the Orishas, representing the highest aspect of divine authority. He is the spiritual father of many other Orishas and serves as a model for moral and ethical behavior. His followers look to him as a source of strength, inspiration, and direction in their spiritual journey.
6. Symbol of divine light: Oxalá represents the divine light that illuminates the path of all beings. He is invoked to bring light into dark situations, dispel confusion, and reveal the truth. In this sense, Oxalá is the guiding force that leads people toward spiritual enlightenment and truth.

The Gypsy or Gitana Spirits

The spirit realm is a sacred and powerful space where we may encounter guides who offer insight, protection, and clarity along our spiritual path. In Brazilian spiritual traditions, one of the most respected and mystically influential groups of guides is known as the Ciganos—a Portuguese word often translated as "Gypsies." While the term "Gypsy" has come under scrutiny in recent years due to its associations with racism and historical abuse against the Romani people, within Brazilian culture it is used with deep reverence. These spirits are honored as powerful entities of divination, intuition, and spiritual wisdom.

In this respectful context, the Ciganos are seen not as caricatures, but as elevated spirit beings closely linked to truth seeking, freedom, and the mastery of psychic gifts. They are often invoked in rituals to bring clarity, reveal hidden truths, and help individuals align with their destiny. Their presence is vibrant, their guidance direct, and their energy deeply transformative.

One of the most beloved figures within this spiritual lineage is Saint Sara, also known as Sara la Kali. She is considered the patron saint of the Ciganos and is venerated with great devotion, especially on May 24. Representing both earthly compassion and spiritual power, Saint Sara is seen as a guardian of those who walk the mystical path. Her story is interwoven with the journey of the Romani people and their spiritual descendants in Brazil, where she is honored for her protection, miracles, and deep maternal energy.

In many spiritual practices, particularly those involving card reading, Saint Sara and the Ciganos play a central role. The Petit Lenormand, for example, is commonly referred to in Brazil as the "Gypsy deck" (Baralho Cigano), due to its widespread use by mediums and intuitive readers who work under the guidance of the Cigano spirits. Adding this historical and cultural layer reminds us of the deck's vibrant spiritual associations, not just as a tool of fortune-telling but as a means of connection with sacred energies.

To walk with the spirits of the Ciganos is to walk with courage, freedom, and faith in one's intuition. Their wisdom, passed down through generations of spiritual contact, continues to illuminate paths for those who seek divine truth and inner liberation.

The Role of Gypsy Spirits in Divination

For practitioners of card reading, especially with the Baralho Cigano, it is commonly believed that one should seek the help of a Gypsy spirit guide to facilitate the readings. The Gypsy spirits are thought to possess an inherent connection to the mystical forces that surround us, making them ideal guides for divination practices. Their wisdom and ability to tap into the energies of the universe can bring clarity, understanding, and valuable insights to the seeker.

A Gypsy spirit guide helps channel messages from the spiritual world, offering guidance on matters such as love, career, health, and personal growth. Their presence is said to enhance the effectiveness of the reading, providing deeper interpretations and clearer answers to the questions posed. The Gypsy spirits are known for their intuitive and often-direct approach, delivering messages in a straightforward yet compassionate manner. This allows the reader to connect with the energy of the cards and tap into the spiritual wisdom that is being shared.

How to Connect with a Gypsy Spirit Guide

To connect with a Gypsy or Gitana spirit guide, one must approach the process with respect, reverence, and an open heart. Many practitioners believe that building a relationship with a Gypsy spirit guide is a gradual process that requires patience and devotion. A few practices that can help establish this connection include the following:

1. Honoring Saint Sara Kali: Saint Sara is regarded as the patroness of all Cigano spirits. Among the vast and vibrant world of Gypsy spirits, Sara la Kali—or Saint Sara—is considered the most powerful and revered. To connect with the Cigano realm, offering devotion and respect to Saint Sara is often seen as the first sacred step. Lighting a candle in her honor on May 24, the day of her celebration, is a meaningful way to invite her protective presence and blessings into your life.
2. Creating sacred space: Gypsy spirits are believed to be deeply connected to the natural world and the mysteries of life. To connect with them, create a sacred space where you can meditate, reflect, and perform divination practices. This space should be quiet, calm, and filled with items that hold significance to the Gypsy spirit world, such as candles, flowers, and incense.
3. Invoking the spirit of the Gypsies: Before performing a card reading or any spiritual practice, invoke the presence of the Gypsy spirit guide. This can be done through prayer, chanting, or simply asking for their assistance with a humble heart. The more you express

gratitude and openness, the more you invite the spirit guides to come forth and provide their wisdom.

4. Using divination tools: Tools such as the Petit Lenormand or other card systems are commonly used in conjunction with the Gypsy spirit guides. As you work with these tools, trust that the spirits will guide you in interpreting the messages and energies that arise during the reading. Be open to the symbols, images, and messages that come through, since they may hold profound meaning for your life.
5. Listening to your intuition: The Gypsy spirits are known for their deep connection to intuition and the unseen world. To fully receive their guidance, it is essential to cultivate your own intuitive abilities. Practice listening to your inner voice, paying attention to subtle signs and synchronicities that may arise as you work with the Gypsy spirits.
6. Invoking the spirit of the Gypsies: Before performing a card reading or any spiritual practice, invoke the presence of the Gypsy spirit guide. This can be done through prayer, chanting, or simply asking for their assistance with a humble heart. The more you express gratitude and openness, the more you invite the spirit guides to come forth and provide their wisdom. The offering of water or libation can also help to attract the Gypsy spirit and facilitate the spiritual engagement.

The Gypsy or Gitana spirits are powerful and compassionate guides, revered for their ability to connect with the spirit world and offer profound wisdom. Saint Sara Kali, as the patron saint of the Gypsies, stands at the center of this spiritual practice, offering protection, guidance, and blessings to all who seek her help. Just as archangel Michael is often seen as the most powerful among the celestial guardians, with other angels acting as guides or companions, Saint Sara holds a similar role among the Cigano spirits. She is the spiritual mother and guide of the entire Cigano lineage, and her presence brings strength, clarity, and deep spiritual insight. By honoring Saint Sara, creating sacred space, and working with divination tools such as the Baralho Cigano, practitioners can deepen their connection to these mystical beings and gain valuable insight into their lives.

In the same way that many angels bear names ending in *-ael* or *-el* (such as Michael, Raphael, Uriel, or Jophiel), the names of Cigano spirits often carry a Romani or eastern European resonance. Well-known spirit names include Cigano Wladimir, Cigano Igor, and Cigana Esmeralda. These names are used with reverence and are always preceded by Cigano (for male) or Cigana (for female) as a sign of honor.

However, it's important to understand that the name of one's personal Cigano or Cigana guide is considered sacred and intimate. Just as we do not always know the true name of our guardian angel, the name of one's Cigano spirit is often kept secret—shared only in moments of deep trust or spiritual revelation. And just as there are countless angels, there are countless Cigano spirits, each with their unique energy, mission, and message.

As you engage with the Gypsy spirits, remember to approach them with respect, reverence, and an open heart, knowing that their guidance will help you navigate life's challenges with clarity, wisdom, and spiritual understanding.

CHAPTER 12

Lenormand Revolution in the United States

For over a century, the Lenormand oracle flourished in Europe, serving as a trusted tool for fortune-telling alongside Tarot cards and traditional playing cards. Yet, despite its rich history, the Lenormand remained relatively unknown in the United States until the 2010s. Around this time, a surge of interest in alternative spiritual practices and divination systems sparked a revolution, bringing this once-obscure oracle into the spotlight.

The rise of the internet and social media played a pivotal role in this transformation. Platforms such as YouTube, Facebook, and later Instagram became hubs where practitioners from all over the world shared their insights, tutorials, and experiences with Lenormand cards. Videos on how to use the cards for divination, discussions on card combinations, and the sharing of real-life readings made Lenormand accessible to a global audience, particularly English-speaking seekers.

American audiences, accustomed to the more introspective and psychological approach of Tarot, were captivated by the directness and precision of Lenormand readings. Its symbolism—simple yet profound—and its ability to provide concrete answers made it an attractive alternative for those looking for clear guidance. This newfound visibility and accessibility turned Lenormand into a fast-growing trend among spiritual enthusiasts, diviners, and even skeptics.

My Journey with Lenormand in the United States

Around the time this revolution was unfolding, one of my young students told me about YouTube, a platform where people could post videos to connect with viewers. She believed I had something unique to offer, and encouraged me to share my knowledge of Lenormand with a wider audience. Whether it was intuition, inspiration, or divine guidance, I decided to give it a try. I recorded and uploaded my first video, not expecting much.

To my surprise, the response was overwhelming. I received an email notifying me that I had reached one thousand followers, and my views were climbing steadily. People began engaging with me, asking for readings, classes, and even a book that could serve as a comprehensive guide to the Lenormand system. Encouraged by their enthusiasm, I began writing my first book, *The Art of Lenormand Reading: Decoding Powerful Messages.* Initially, finding a publisher was a challenge. The responses were disheartening: "There's no place in our catalog for this kind of material." But the cards guided me, as they always had, to take matters into my own hands. I used my savings to self-publish six thousand copies. When the delivery truck unloaded stacks of books into my garage, the enormity of the task hit me—how would I sell all these books?

Four months later, every copy had been sold. This success caught the attention of Schiffer Publishing, who agreed to publish the book, giving it the reach and distribution it deserved.

As Lenormand gained traction in the United States, its use began to evolve. Practitioners integrated their own cultural and spiritual traditions into readings, blending Lenormand with methods such as intuitive divination, astrology, and even modern psychology.

Workshops, conferences, and online courses dedicated to Lenormand began popping up, and American authors started writing books tailored to a Western audience. Deck creators also emerged, crafting Lenormand decks that reflected diverse artistic styles and themes, making the cards even more appealing to a modern audience.

Unlike Tarot, which often delves into philosophical or psychological depths, Lenormand was appreciated for its practical, everyday applications. Questions about relationships, career decisions, and financial matters found straightforward answers through its symbols. Social media transformed Lenormand into a community-driven movement. American readers began sharing their techniques, creating new spreads, and exploring hybrid systems. Facebook groups and Instagram accounts dedicated to Lenormand exploded in popularity, allowing enthusiasts to connect, learn, and share their insights. Online marketplaces such as Etsy and independent publishers provided platforms for artists and creators to produce unique Lenormand decks. These decks often incorporated modern aesthetics, cultural symbolism, and innovations that resonated with a new generation of readers.

The hunger for knowledge among Lenormand enthusiasts in the United States is unparalleled. Americans are still exploring the depths of this system, often going further into research than their European counterparts. This passion has led to incredible discoveries about Lenormand's history, techniques, and cultural significance. It is a blessing to witness such dedication, and this enthusiasm creates opportunities for authors, teachers, and mentors to share their vast knowledge and experience. The Lenormand deck holds endless possibilities, and its ability to adapt to various cultures and practices ensures that its legacy will continue to grow. Together, we have the privilege of guiding this ongoing revolution and helping even more people connect with the powerful messages of this oracle.

Today, Lenormand continues to thrive in the United States, standing as both a divination tool and a cultural bridge between Europe and the Americas. Its journey from obscurity to prominence highlights the power of connection and the universal human desire for guidance, clarity, and a deeper understanding of life's mysteries.

Lenormand's rise is a testament to how ancient wisdom can find new relevance in modern times—and how a humble deck of cards can inspire a revolution.

CHAPTER 13

Lenormand's Dawn in the Land Where the Sun Rises

The Lenormand revolution continues to expand, and Asia has become one of the newest frontiers in the oracle's global journey. After the remarkable success of Lenormand in the United States, its popularity transcended Western borders, captivating diviners and spiritual seekers across Asia. This region, rich in diverse cultures and ancient traditions, has warmly embraced Lenormand, adapting it in unique ways while honoring its European roots.

In recent years, the interconnectedness brought by the internet and social media has played a critical role in introducing Lenormand to Asia. Online platforms exposed Asian audiences to the oracle's rich symbolism, concise readings, and practical applications. Videos showcasing Lenormand spreads and interpretations sparked curiosity, while workshops and webinars made learning accessible to a broader audience. Asia's spiritual seekers, often steeped in systems such as feng shui, I Ching, and astrology, were drawn to the straightforward nature of Lenormand. Its ability to provide precise answers resonated deeply, and its practical focus on life's everyday questions—relationships, finances, career—aligned well with the pragmatic aspects of many Asian spiritual practices.

I've had the privilege of teaching Lenormand in countries such as Thailand and China, and the experience has been nothing short of transformative. From the moment I began introducing the cards to students, I noticed a deep enthusiasm and hunger for knowledge. Asian learners approach Lenormand with a level of dedication that is both inspiring and humbling.

In Thailand, where spirituality is interwoven with daily life, students were fascinated by how Lenormand could blend with their own intuitive practices. They drew parallels between Lenormand's symbols and the imagery found in their own cultural and religious traditions, creating a bridge between the familiar and the new.

In China, the response was equally remarkable. Chinese students, accustomed to systems such as the I Ching or face reading, appreciated Lenormand's structured yet accessible nature. They approached the cards with meticulous attention to detail, exploring how the combinations worked and marveling at the oracle's precision.

The appeal of Lenormand in Asia lies in its adaptability. The oracle is simple enough to be understood quickly, but profound enough to provide layered insights. Its straightforward symbolism resonates with Asian divination traditions, which often emphasize clarity and practical guidance.

What truly sets Lenormand apart is its universality. The cards can be used independently or blended with local practices, creating a fusion of Western and Eastern spirituality. For example:

- In Japan, where Tarot already has a dedicated following, Lenormand has found a niche among those seeking faster and more-direct answers.
- In India, practitioners are exploring connections among Lenormand, Vedic astrology, deities, and spiritual beings, discovering how the cards can complement astrological readings.

The growing interest in Lenormand across Asia signals a bright future for this oracle. Just as Lenormand adapted to the cultural landscapes of Europe and the Americas, it is now being transformed by Asian practitioners. This cross-cultural exchange is a testament to Lenormand's flexibility and enduring appeal.

Asia's dedication to learning and innovation ensures that Lenormand will continue to thrive in the region. With each workshop, class, and reading, a new generation of practitioners is discovering the magic of this oracle, exploring its endless possibilities, and adding their unique perspectives to its legacy. I am so curious and excited to see where this new blend of ideas will lead.

As a teacher and author, I feel honored to witness this evolution first-hand. The enthusiasm of Asian students reaffirms that Lenormand is more than just a deck of cards—it is a universal language of guidance, connection, and wisdom. And as the oracle continues its journey across continents, one thing is clear: The Lenormand revolution is far from over. Which country will be next?

As a special feature of this book, you'll find a mini Lenormand deck included—designed to accompany you wherever your intuition calls. This compact format allows you to easily practice readings on the go, lay quick daily spreads, or deepen your connection to the symbols through regular use. Whether you're pulling a single card for guidance or exploring a full spread like the Grand Tableau, this mini deck invites you to bring the Lenormand language into your everyday life with ease and intention. Whether you are a seasoned Lenormand reader or a curious beginner, this book will open your mind to the fascinating ways in which these cards serve as bridges between intuition, culture, and divination.